The '

and Other Poems

The Testament

and Other Poems

François Villon

Translated by Anthony Mortimer

ALMA CLASSICS

ALMA CLASSICS
an imprint of

ALMA BOOKS LTD
Thornton House
Thornton Road
Wimbledon Village
London SW19 4NG
United Kingdom
www.almaclassics.com

First published by Alma Classics Ltd in 2013
This new, revised edition first published by Alma Classics in 2023

Translation, Notes, Extra Material © Anthony Mortimer 2013, 2023

Printed and bound by CPI Group (UK) Ltd, Croydon, CR0 4YY

ISBN: 978-1-84749-899-1

Contents

For Martin Dodsworth

Bienfait ne se doit oublier

The Testament
and Other Poems

The Legacy

(*Le Lais François Villon*)

1   L'an quatre cens cinquante six,
       Je, Françoys Villon, escollier,
       Considerant, de sens rassis,
       Le frain aux dens, franc au collier,
       Qu'on doit ses euvres conseillier,
       Come Vegece le racompte,
       Saige Rommain, grant conseillier,
       Ou autrement on se mescompte…

2   En ce temps que j'ay dit devant,
       Sur le Noël, morte saison,
       Que les loups se vivent du vent
       Et qu'on se tient en sa maison,
       Pour le frimas, près du tyson,
       Me vint ung vouloir de briser
       La très amoureuse prison
       Qui faisoit mon cueur debriser.

3   Je le feiz en telle façon,
       Voyant celle devant mes yeulx
       Consentant à ma deffaçon,
       Sans ce que ja luy en fust mieulx ;
       Dont je me dueil et plains aux cieulx,
       En requerant d'elle vengence
       A tous les dieux venerïeux,
       Et du grief d'amours allegence.

4   Et se j'ay prins en ma faveur
       Ses doulx regars et beaux semblans
       De très decevante saveur,
       Me tresparsans jusques aux flans…
       Bien ils ont vers moy les piés blancs
       Et me faillent au grant besoing,
       Planter me fault aultres complans
       Et frapper en ung aultre coing.

1   In fourteen fifty-six, the year
     When I, a scholar, François Villon,
     Being sound of mind, with senses clear,
     Champing the bit, keen to be gone,
     Knowing one should reflect upon
     One's works – or so Vegetius states
     (Sage counsellor and Rome's great son) –
     Otherwise one miscalculates…

2   In that dead season, as I say,
     About the time when Christ was born,   10
     When wolves drink wind, and wise men stay
     Indoors because the frost is keen,
     And blow on logs to make them burn,
     The urge came on me to break out
     From the harsh prison where love's chain
     Had shackled my poor broken heart.*

3   This then was how it came to be:
     I thought she stood before my eyes,
     Consenting to my fall, though she
     Gained nothing good from my demise: 20
     So that I raised my woeful cries
     To the venereal gods above,
     Imploring vengeance from the skies,
     Relief from all the pains of love.

4   And if I took as signs of favour
     Her smiles and glances on the sly
     That pierced with their deceptive flavour
     Deep to the marrow of my thigh,
     They turn and leave me high and dry
     In my great hour of need: so now   30
     I'll mint upon another die
     And look for some fresh field to plough.

5

5   Le regart de celle m'a prins
       Qui m'a esté felonne et dure :
       Sans ce qu'en riens j'aye mesprins,
       Veult et ordonne que j'endure
       La mort et que plus je ne dure.
       Si n'y vois secours que fouïr :
       Rompre veult la vive soudure
       Sans mes piteulx regretz ouïr.

6   Pour obvier à ces dangers,
       Mon mieulx est, ce croy, de partir.
       A Dieu ! Je m'en vois à Angers.
       Puis qu'el ne me veult impartir
       Sa grace, il me convient partir :
       Par elle meurs, les menbres sains.
       Au fort, je suys amant martir
       Du nombre des amoureux sains.

7   Combien que le depart me soit
       Dur, si fault il que je l'eslongne :
       Comme mon povre sens consoit,
       Aultre que moy est en quelongne,
       Dont oncques soret de Boulongne
       Ne fut plus alteré d'humeur.
       C'est pour moy piteuse besongne :
       Dieu en veuille ouÿr ma clameur !

8   Et puys que departir me fault
       Et du retour ne suys certain
       (Je ne suys homme sans deffault,
       Ne qu'aultre d'assier ne d'estain :
       Vivre aux humains est incertain
       Et après mort n'y a relaiz)
       Je m'en vois en pays lointain,
       Si establis ce present laiz.

5   One glance from her brought on the great
     And harsh injustice I endure;
     Nothing I've done deserved this fate,
     Yet she's determined to ensure
     That I should die, and there's no cure
     That I can see except in flight:
     She breaks our living bond; what's more,
     She's deaf when I lament my plight.   40

6   With all these risks, it might be well
     To simply take my leave, and so
     Here's off to Angers and farewell!
     For, after all, since she won't show
     Me any favour, I should go:
     She kills me, though I'm strong and sound –
     In short, a martyr here below
     Among the saints that Love has crowned.

7   However hard it is to quit
     Her presence, still I'll have to leave: 50
     It's pretty clear to my poor wit
     Some other distaff helps her weave;
     Thirst such as salted herrings give
     She has for him, but not for me.
     It's a bad business, I believe:
     May the Lord listen to my plea!

8   And since it's clear I must be off,
     And my return is far from sure –
     I'm just a man, not made of stuff
     Like steel or tin without a flaw: 60
     All human life is most unsure:
     Once dead, you can't give much away
     And I'll be on a distant shore –
     I now make out this Legacy.

9   Premierement, ou nom du Pere,
          Du Filz et du Saint Esperit,
          Et de sa glorïeuse Mere
          Par qui grace rien ne perit,
          Je laisse, de par Dieu, mon bruyt
          A maistre Guillaume Villon,
          Qui en l'onneur de son nom bruyt,
          Mes tentes et mon pavillon.

10   Item, à celle que j'ay dit,
          Qui si durement m'a chassé
          Que je suis de joye interdit
          Et de tout plaisir dechassé,
          Je laisse mon cueur enchassé,
          Palle, piteux, mort et transy.
          Elle m'a ce mal pourchassé,
          Mais Dieu luy en face mercy !

11   Item, à maistre Ytier Marchant,
          Auquel je me sens très tenu,
          Laisse mon branc d'acier tranchant
          — Et à maistre Jehan le Cornu —
          Qui est en gaige detenu
          Pour ung escot sept solz montant ;
          Je veul, selon le contenu,
          Qu'on leur livre — en le rachetant !

12   Item, je laisse à Sainct Amant
          Le Cheval blanc avec *la Mule*,
          Et à Blaru mon dÿamant
          Et l'*Asne royé* qui recule.
          Et le decret qui articule
          Omnis utriusque sexus
          Contre la Carmeliste bulle
          Laisse aux curés, pour mettre sus.

9   First, in the name of God the Father,
With both the Son and Holy Ghost,
Together with His Glorious Mother,
Thanks to whose grace no soul is lost,
I leave what fame I have to rest
With that good man Guillaume Villon   70
(To honour his fair name, I trust)
And also my pavilion.*

10   Item, to her of whom I've spoken
Who cast me off with such deep spite
That I was left quite joyless, broken,
Exiled from pleasure and delight,
I leave a casket with my heart
Piteous, pale, and stiff and dead.
She sought my ruin with this blight,
But may God pardon what she did!   80

11   Item, my blade of good sharp steel
To Master Ythier Marchant, who
Leaves me in debt to him, I feel –
Let him go shares with Jean Cornu.
A tavern bill of seven sous
Means that right now the thing's in hock.
Hereby I state that it's their due,
Provided they can buy it back.

12   Item, I leave to Saint-Amant
Two signs, *The White Horse* and *The Mule*,*   90
And to Blaru my diamond
And *The Striped Ass* that's hard to rule.
Then the decretal made to spell
Omnis utriusque sexus
I leave (despite the Carmelite Bull)*
To parish priests who should confess us.

13   Et à maistre Robert Valée,
      Povre clergon en Parlement,
      Qui n'entent ne mont ne valée,
      J'ordonne principalement
      Qu'on luy baille legierement
      Mes brayes, estans aux *Trumillieres*,
      Pour coyffer plus honnestement
      S'amye Jehanne de Millieres.

14   Pour ce qu'il est de lieu honneste,
      Fault qu'il soit mieulx recompensé,
      Car le Saint Esprit l'admoneste,
      Obstant ce qu'il est insensé ;
      Pour ce, je me suis pourpensé,
      Puis qu'il n'a sens ne qu'une aulmoire,
      De recouvrer sur Mau Pensé,
      Qu'on luy baille, l'*Art de memoire*.

15   Item, pour assigner la vie
      Du dessus dit maistre Robert
      (Pour Dieu, n'y aiés point d'envye !) ;
      Mes parens, vendés mon haubert
      Et que l'argent, ou la plus part,
      Soit emploié dedens ces Pasques
      A acheter à ce poupart
      Une fenestre emprès Sainct Jacques.

16   Item, laisse et donne en pur don
      Mes gans et ma houcque de soye
      A mon amy Jacques Cardon,
      Le glan aussi d'une saulsoye,
      Et tous les jours une grasse oye
      Et ung chappon de haulte gresse,
      Dix muys de vin blanc comme croye
      Et deux procés, que trop n'engresse.

13   Master Robert Valée (or Vale),
Poor little clerk to Parlement,
Who still can't tell a hill from dale:
Without delay I'd have him sent   100
My underpants: he should present
Them straight to Jeanne de Millières,
His girlfriend, for this gift is meant
As the best headdress she could wear.

14   Because he's of good stock, he'd merit
Some greater recompense, as is right,
By order of the Holy Spirit,
Although he isn't very bright;
So off to Malpensé, I thought,
(Since there's no cupboard quite so thick)   110
And there I'll buy for him *The Art
Of Memory* to help things stick.

15   Item, because he needs to make
A living, this same Master Vale,
(Don't envy him, for Heaven's sake!)
Dear kinsmen, flog my coat of mail
And use the profits from the sale
To buy the kid a scrivener's perch –
Do it by Easter without fail! –
Some window by St James's church.   120

16   I'll leave to Jacques Cardon, my friend,
My hooded silken cape and gloves
And with this outright gift, I'll send
Acorns that fall in willow groves,
A fat goose over and above,
With a fat capon: after that,
Some chalky wine – but still he'll have
Two lawsuits to keep down the fat.

17 Item, je lesse à ce jeune homme,
  Regnier de Montigny, trois chiens,
  Aussi à Jehan Raguier la somme
  De cent francs prins sur tous mes biens.
  Mais quoy ? Je n'y comprens en riens
  Ce que je pourray acquerir :
  L'en ne doit trop prendre des siens,
  Ne trop ses amys surquerir.

18 Item, au seigneur de Grigny
  Laisse la garde de Nygon
  Et six chiens plus qu'à Montigny,
  Vicestre, chastel et donjon,
  Et à ce malostru changon,
  Mouton, qui le tient en procés,
  Laisse troys coups d'un escourgon
  Et coucher paix et aise es ceps.

19 Item, au Chevalier du guet,
  Le Hëaulme luy establis,
  Et aux pietons qui vont d'aguet
  Tastonnans par ces establis,
  Je leur laissë ung beau riblis :
  La Lanterne à la Pierre au Let ;
  Voire, mes j'aray *les Troys Lis*,
  S'ilz me mainent en Chastellet.

20 Et à maistre Jacques Raguier
  Laisse l'Abeuvroir Popin,
  Perches, poussins au blanc menger,
  Tous jours le choiz d'un bon loppin,
  Le trou de *la Pomme de Pin*,
  Cloz et couvert, au feu la plante,
  Enmaillotté en jacopin ;
  Et qui vouldra planter, si plante !

17   Three dogs for young de Montigny
       I hereby promise and donate;   130
       And for Jean Raguier there'll be
       A hundred francs from my estate.
       Hold on! I don't include in that
       My future earnings. It's a sin
       To ask too much of your best mates
       Or take too much from your own kin.

18   I leave the Seigneur de Grigny
       The guard of Nijon's stony heap,*
       And six dogs more than Montigny,
       Bicêtre too, castle and keep.   140
       And to the devil's spawn, that creep
       Mouton, who's taken him to court,
       Some leg-irons for a long sweet sleep
       And three good leatherings, just in sport.

19   Item, the Night Watch has a knight*
       Who gets *The Helm*; for the patrol
       I've nicked a trophy that's just right
       To help them grope round shop and stall:
       The Lantern near the prison wall!
       And if I'm nicked myself, I say,   150
       *Three Lily Buds** will give me all
       My bed and board at Châtelet.

20   Item, to Master Jacques Raguier
       I leave the Popin watering place;
       They've some nice titbits every day,
       Perch, pullets cooked in almond sauce:
       But at *The Pine Cone's* fire of course,
       Cosy and close, he warms his heels,
       Gowned like a friar (though not so coarse):
       Let every ploughman plough his field!*   160

21   Item, à maistre Jehan Mautaint
Et maistre Pierre Basannier,
Le gré du seigneur qui attainct
Troubles, forfaiz, sans espargnier ;
Et à mon procureur Fournier,
Bonnetz cours, chausses semelées,
Taillées sur mon cordouennier,
Pour porter durant ces gelées.

22   Item, à Jehan Trouvé, boucher,
Laisse *le Mouton* franc et tendre,
Et ung tacon pour esmouchier
Le Beuf Couronné qu'on veult vendre,
Et *la Vache*, qui pourra prendre
Le villain qui la trousse au col :
S'il ne la rend, qu'on le puist pendre
Et estrangler d'un bon licol !

23   Item, à Perrenet Marchant,
Qu'on dit le Bastard de la Barre,
Pour ce qu'il est ung bon marchant,
Luy laisse troys gluyons de feurre
Pour estendre dessus la terre
A faire l'amoureux mestier,
Où il luy fauldra sa vie querre,
Car il ne scet autre mestier.

24   Item, au Loup et à Cholet
Je laisse à la foys ung canart
Prins sur les murs comme on souloit,
Envers les fossés, sur le tart,
Et à chacun ung grant tabart
De cordelier jusques aux piez,
Busche, charbon, des poys au lart
Et mes houseaulx sans avanpiez.

21   Item, to Master Jean Mautaint
      And Master Pierre Basannier
      The grace of that lord* who comes down
      On brawls and crimes without delay;
      And to my lawyer Fournier
      Tight caps and socks with slipper soles,*
      My cobbler's work, to wear today
      Against the frost and icy cold.

22   And to the butcher Jean Trouvé,
      I leave *The Sheep*, fine tender stuff;   170
      A whisk to drive the flies away
      From *The Crowned Ox* they're selling off;
      The Cow, if we can catch the thief
      Who picked her up; and let's not falter:
      If he won't give her back, get tough
      And strangle him with his own halter.

23   Item, to Perrenet Marchant,*
      Known as the Bastard de la Barre,
      Since doing business is his bent,
      I hereby leave three bales of straw,   180
      So he can spread it on the floor
      Where all his amorous deals are made;
      His living comes from such affairs
      Because he knows no other trade.

24   Item, to Loup and to Cholet,*
      The pair of them, I leave a duck
      Caught on the walls in the old way,
      By moats at night, if you're in luck;
      Each gets a long Franciscan cloak
      That reaches down from head to foot,   190
      Firewood, coal, and peas with pork,
      And then my toeless boots to boot.

25   Item, je lessë en pitié
A troys petis enffans tous nudz
Nommés en ce present traictié,
Povres orphelins inpourveuz,
Tous deschaussez, tous despourveuz
Et desnuez comme le ver
— J'ordonne qu'ilz seront pourveuz,
Au moins pour passer cest yver :

26   Premierement Colin Laurens,
Girard Gossuïn, Jehan Marceau,
Desprins de biens et de parens,
Qui n'ont vaillant l'anse d'un seau,
Chacun de mes biens ung fesseau
Ou quatre blancs, s'ilz l'aiment mieulx.
Ilz mengeront maint bon morseau,
Les enffans, quant je seray vieulx.

27   Item, ma nominacïon
Que j'ay de l'Université
Laisse par resignacïon
Pour seclurre d'adversité
Povres clercs de ceste cité
Soubz cest *intendit* contenus ;
Charité m'y a incité
Et Nature, les voyans nudz.

28   C'est maistre Guillaume Cottin
Et maistre Thibault de Vittry,
Deux povres clercs parlans latin,
Humbles, bien chantans au lectry,
Paisibles enffans sans estry :
Je leur laisse sans recevoir
Sur la maison Guillot Gueutry,
En attendant de mieulx avoir.

25   Item, my pity's vast extent
Would cover three small naked lads,
Named in the present document,
Poor orphans* who have lost their dad,
All barefoot, destitute and sad,
And mother-naked every one –
I order they be fed and clad
At least until the winter's done.   200

26   At Colin Laurens I begin,
Then Girard Gossuin, Jean Marceau;
With neither property nor kin,
They couldn't buy a bucket: so
Four farthings each – it's that, or go
Away with all that they can hold
Of what was mine. These lads, I know
Will make a meal when I am old.*

27   Next item is my nomination*
Sealed by the University,   210
I leave it, with my resignation,
To shelter from adversity
Some clerks residing in this city;
Whose names I have included here:
It's Charity that moves my pity
And Nature, seeing them go bare.

28   I mean Master Guillaume Cotin
And Master Thibaud de Vitry,
Two humble clerks* who know their Latin
Enough to chant the liturgy,   220
Peaceful young chaps and trouble-free;
I leave them rent that's in arrears,
Still owing from Guillot Gueutry,
Until some better bet appears.

29   Item, et j'adjoinctz à la crosse
        Celle de la rue Saint Anthoine,
        Ou ung billart de quoy on crosse
        Et tous les jours plain pot de Seine ;
        Au pigons qui sont en l'essoyne
        Enserrés soubz trappe voliere,
        Mon mirouër bel et ydoine,
        Et la grace de la geolliere.

30   Item, je lesse aux hospitaux
        Mes chassis tissus d'arignie,
        Et aux gisans soubz les estaulx
        Chacun sur l'eul une grongnée,
        Trambler à chiere renfrongnée,
        Megres, velus et morfondus,
        Chausses courtes, robe rongnée,
        Gelez, murdriz et enfondus.

31   Item, je laisse à mon barbier
        Les rongneures de mes cheveux,
        Plainement et sans destourbier,
        Au savetier mes soulliers vieulx,
        Et au freppier mes habitz tieulx
        Que quant du tout je les delesse.
        Pour mains qu'ilz ne cousterent neufz
        Charitablement je leur lesse.

32   Item, je laisse aux Mendïans,
        Aux Filles Dieu et aux Beguines,
        Savoureux morceaulx et fryans,
        Chappons, flaons, grasses gelines,
        Et puis prescher les Quinze Signes
        Et abatre pain à deux mains.
        Carmes chevauchent noz voisines,
        Mais cela, ce n'est que du mains.

29   If not a crook, I add a cross*
From rue Saint-Antoine as a sign,
The billiard cue supplants the cross,
Seine water's healthier than wine;
To jailbirds who must peak and pine,
Cribbed, cabined and confined for life,   230
I leave this mirror clear and fine,
And favour from the jailer's wife.

30   The poorhouses inherit all
My precious cobwebbed window panes;
Dropouts who sleep in market stalls
Get each a black eye for their pains;
Now let them shiver, faces drained,
Stubbly, coughing, cold and thin,
With hose too short and tattered gown,
Frozen and battered, soaked to the skin.   240

31   I grant my barber without let
Or hindrance the last locks of hair
Cut from my head; the cobbler gets
The shabby shoes I used to wear.
The ragman too will have his share
Of cast-offs for a modest fee –
Less than when new is only fair,
And that's what I call charity!

32   Item, I leave to Mendicant Friars,
Béguines and Daughters of the Lord,   250
All that a hungry soul desires,
Tarts, pies and capons, hens full-fed;
The right to pocket piles of bread
And preach the Final Fifteen Signs.*
(The Carmelites ride our wives instead,
But that's the least of their designs.)

33   Item, laisse *le Mortier d'Or*
A Jehan, l'espicier, de la Garde,
Une potence de sainct Mor
Pour faire ung broyer à moustarde.
Et celluy qui fist l'avangarde
Pour faire sur moy griefz exploiz,
De par moy, saint Anthoine l'arde !
Je ne lui feray autre laiz.

34   Item, je lesse à Mirebeuf
Et à Nicolas de Louviers,
A chacun l'escaille d'un oeuf
Plaine de francs et d'escus vieulx.
Quant au concierge de Gouvieulx,
Pierre de Rousseville, ordonne
Pour le donner entendre mieulx,
Escus telz que le Prince donne.

35   Finablement, en escripvant,
Ce soir, seulet, estant en bonne,
Dictant ces laiz et descripvant,
J'ouys la cloche de Serbonne,
Qui tous jours a neuf heures sonne
Le Salut que l'Ange predit ;
Si suspendis et mis en bonne
Pour prier comme le cueur dit.

36   Ce faisant, je m'entroubliay,
Non pas par force de vin boire,
Mon esperit comme lyé.
Lors je sentis Dame Memoire
Reprendre et mectre en son aulmoire
Ses especes colaterales,
Oppinative faulse et voire,
Et autres intellectualles,

33   I leave the grocer de la Garde
      The Golden Mortar, and, as pestle,
      A Saint Maur's crutch that's long and hard
      To grind his mustard in that vessel.   260
      As for the one whose hate and hassle
      Set off such vile assaults on me,*
      St Anthony's Fire* is all I'll settle
      On him in this my legacy!

34   Item, I leave to Mirebeuf
      And Nicholas de Louvieux too
      An eggshell each that's just enough
      When filled with francs and old *écus*:
      And to the Warden Rousseville, who
      Keeps watch at Gouvieux by the pool   270
      (To help him understand what's due),
      Coin minted by the Prince of Fools.

35   At last, while here alone tonight,
      I felt a cheerful mood come on,
      And as I wrote this legacy out,
      I heard the bell of the Sorbonne
      Which just at nine each evening sounds
      The Angelus; and, for my part,
      I paused and put my writing down
      To pray directly from the heart.   280

36   At this, I fell into a trance,*
      Not because wine befuddled me:
      My mind seemed bound, as in suspense
      Until I felt Dame Memory
      Take back and shelve where they should be
      Her species classed collateral,
      Opinative, both false and true
      And others intellectual,

37   Et meismement l'estimative,
        Par quoy prospective nous vient,
        Simulative, formative,
        Desquelles souvent il advient
        Que, par leur trouble, homme devient
        Fol et lunatique par moys :
        Je l'ay lu, se bien m'en souvient,
        En Aristote aucunes fois.

38   Dont le sensitif s'esveilla
        Et esvertua Fantasie,
        Qui les organes resveilla
        Et tint la souveraine partie
        En suspens et comme mortie
        Par oppressïon d'oubliance,
        Qui en moy s'estoit espartie
        Pour monstrer de Sens la lïance.

39   Puis que mon sens fut à repos
        Et l'entendement desmellé,
        Je cuiday finer mon propos,
        Mais mon ancrë estoit gelé
        Et mon cierge trouvay soufflé ;
        De feu je n'eusse peu finer.
        Si m'endormis, tout emmouflé,
        Et ne peuz autrement finer.

40   Fait au temps de ladite datte
        Par le bon renommé Villon,
        Qui ne mengue figue ne datte,
        Sec et noir comme escouvillon :
        Il n'a tente ne pavillon
        Qu'il n'ait lessié à ses amis,
        Et n'a mais qu'un peu de billon
        Qui sera tantost à fin mis.

37   And likewise the estimative
      Which shows the probable to us,   290
      The simulative and formative,
      Which, if disturbed, can cause a fuss
      That sends a man delirious
      And crazy once a month. The wise
      Old Aristotle put it thus –
      I must have read it once or twice.

38   So then the sensory came and broke
      The sleep of my wild Fantasy
      That stirred the organs, which awoke,
      Causing the sovereign faculty,   300
      Reason, to lose authority;
      Oblivion held it mute, confined,
      Oppressing every part of me
      To show the bondage of the mind.

39   My mind once calm again and sound,
      My understanding cleared of doubt,
      I thought to finish off, but found
      My ink was frozen in the pot
      And my poor candle had blown out;
      I couldn't find a light just then,   310
      But fell asleep, wrapped in my coat,
      And failed to make a fitting end.

40   Made here upon the given date
      By Villon, man of fair renown,
      Who doesn't glut on figs or dates,
      Whose moplike head is dry and brown:
      There's no pavilion that's his own
      Or tent not settled on a friend;
      What little cash he hasn't blown
      Will very soon come to an end.   320

The Testament
(*Le Testament Villon*)

1   En l'an de mon trentiesme aage,
     Que toutes mes hontes j'euz beues,
     Ne du tout fol, ne du tout saige,
     Non obstant maintes peines eues,
     Lesquelles j'ay toutes receues
     Soubz la main Thibault d'Aucigny —
     S'esveque il est, signant les rues,
     Qu'il soit le mien, je le regny.

2   Mon seigneur n'est ne mon evesque.
     Soubz luy ne tiens s'il n'est en friche,
     Foy ne luy doy n'ommaige avecque :
     Je ne suis son serf ne sa biche.
     Peu m'a d'une petite miche
     Et de froide eaue tout ung esté ;
     Large ou estroit, moult me fut chiche :
     Tel luy soit Dieu qu'il m'a esté !

3   Et s'aucun me vouloit reprendre
     Et dire que je le mauldiz,
     Non faiz, se bien me scet comprendre ;
     En rien de luy je ne mesdiz.
     Vecy tout le mal que j'en dis :
     S'il m'a esté misericors,
     Jhesus, le roy de paradis,
     Tel luy soit à l'ame et au corps !

4   Et s'esté m'a dur ne cruel
     Trop plus que cy je ne raconte,
     Je veul que le Dieu eternel
     Luy soit dont semblable à ce compte .
     Et l'Eglise nous dit et compte
     Que prions pour noz annemys ;
     Je vous dis que j'ay tort et honte,
     Quoy qu'il m'aist fait, à Dieu remys.

1   Being in my thirtieth year of life
       And having swallowed shame on shame,
       Not quite a fool and yet not wise,
       Despite the many pains that came
       To me from one who bears the name
       Of Bishop Thibaud d'Aussigny – *
       He blesses streets, but all the same,
       That he's my bishop I deny.

2   He's not my bishop, not my lord,
       What land I hold from him lies bare,   10
       I pledged no homage, gave no word;
       I'm not his hind, his little deer;*
       I spent one summer in his care –
       One bun a day, cold water free:
       Say what you like, that's wretched fare;
       May God treat him as he did me!

3   And if somebody wants to call
       What I have said a dreadful curse,
       Not so: I speak no ill at all
       Of him, if you can grasp my case.   20
       Here's what I say, and nothing worse:
       If mercy's what he showed me then,
       May Christ with that same mercy grace
       His soul and body in their turn!

4   And if he's been so harsh and hard,
       Far more than I can ever tell,
       I only wish the eternal God
       Would settle his account so well.
       The Church insists that we should still
       Pray even for our enemy;   30
       I suffered wrong and shame, yet will
       Let God judge what he did to me.

5   Si prieray pour luy de bon cueur,
     Pour l'ame du bon feu Cotart ;
     Mais quoy ? ce sera donc par cueur,
     Car de lire je suis fetart.
     Priere en feray de Picart.
     S'il ne le scet, voise l'apprendre,
     S'il m'en croit, ains qu'il soit plus tart,
     A Douay ou à L'Ysle en Flandre.

6   Combien, s'oÿr veult qu'on prie
     Pour luy, foy que doy mon baptesme,
     Obstant qu'à chacun ne le crye,
     Il ne fauldra pas à son esme :
     Ou psaultier prens, quant suis à mesme,
     Qui n'est de beuf ne cordouen,
     Le verselet escript septiesme
     Du psëaume *Deus laudem.*

7   Si prie au benoist filz de Dieu,
     Qu'à tous mes besoings je reclame,
     Que ma povre priere ait lieu
     Vers Luy, de qui tiens corps et ame,
     Qui m'a preservé de maint blasme
     Et franchy de ville puissance :
     Loué soit Il, et Nostre Dame,
     Et Loÿs, le bon roy de France.

8   Auquel doint Dieu l'eur de Jacob
     Et de Salmon l'onneur et gloire
     (Quant de prouesse, il en a trop,
     De force aussi, par m'ame, voire !)
     En ce monde cy transsitoire,
     Tant qu'il a de long ne de lé,
     Afin que de lui soit memoire,
     Vivre autant que Mathussalé.

5 Still, by the soul of old Cotart,
  My prayer will be sincere and true,
  Coming, believe me, from the heart –
  I'm far too lax to read one through.
  I'll pray for him as Picards do,*
  A prayer that he should learn, I feel,
  While there's still time, by going to
  Some Flanders town, Douai or Lille.   40

6 Yet if he wants to hear me pray
  For him, then by the faith I got
  Baptized in, he shall have his way,
  Although I won't exactly shout:
  One day I'll take my psalter out,
  Not bound in hide or cordovan,
  And open it at just about
  The *Deus laudem*, say verse seven.*

7 I beg God's blessed Son, on whom
  In every need I call and cry,   50
  From whom my soul and body come,
  That my poor prayer may rise on high
  To Him who saved and set me free
  From evil power and such mischance:
  All praise to Him, and Our Lady,
  And Louis, the good King of France.*

8 Now may God grant him Jacob's luck,
  Solomon's honour and his glory
  (In prowess he's not out of stock,
  Strength too, my soul! you know the story); 60
  Throughout this world so transitory,
  Its length and breadth, both near and far,
  May God assure his memory
  With lifespan like Methuselah.

9   Et douze beaux enffans, tous masles,
     Vëoir de son cher sang royal,
     Aussi preux que fut le grant Charles,
     Conceuz en ventre nuptïal,
     Bons comme fut saint Marcïal.
     Ainsi en preigne au feu Daulphin !
     Je ne lui soubzhaicte autre mal,
     Et puis paradis en la fin.

10   Pour ce que foible je me sens
     Trop plus de biens que de sancté,
     Tant que je suis en mon plain sens,
     Sy peu que Dieu m'en a presté,
     Car d'autre ne l'ay emprunté —,
     J'ay ce testament très estable
     Fait, de derreniere voulenté,
     Seul pour tout et inrevocable,

11   Et escript l'an soixante et ung,
     Lors que le roy me delivra
     De la dure prison de Mehun
     Et que vie me recouvra,
     Dont suis, tant que mon cueur vivra,
     Tenu vers luy m'usmilier,
     Ce que feray jusqu'il moura :
     Bienfait ne se doit oublier.

12   Or est vray qu'après plains et pleurs
     Et angoisseux gemissemens,
     Après tritresses et douleurs,
     Labours et griefz cheminemens,
     Travail mes lubres sentemens,
     Esguisez comme une pelocte,
     M'ouvrist plus que tous les commens
     D'Averroÿs sur Arristote.

9   And may a dozen children come
     (All sons) from his dear royal blood,
     Conceived in holy nuptial womb,
     Brave like our Charlemagne, and good
     As was St Martial, so it's said.
     May our late Dauphin have all this!   70
     I wish him nothing worse, but add:
     Let Paradise at last be his.

10   Since I feel poor and far declined
     (In goods and not in health, I own)
     While I possess what little mind
     The Lord has lent, that's mine alone
     (I owe to no one else that loan),
     I've made a testament that shall
     Fix my last wishes, as in stone,
     Definitive, once and for all,   80

11   Written in this year Sixty-One,
     When the good king delivered me
     From vile imprisonment at Meung,
     Restored my life and set me free,
     For which my heart shall ever be
     Bound to him until death, and set
     To serve him with humility,
     For no good deed should be forgot.

12   Now true it is that after groans,
     Tears and complaints about my load,   90
     Sadness and sobs and bitter moans
     And toilsome days upon the road,
     This suffering opened my dull head
     (Sharp as a ball of wool) to subtle
     Truths more than Averroës showed
     In comments upon Aristotle.

13   Combien, au plus fort de mes maulx,
En cheminant sans croix ne pille,
Dieu, qui les pelerins d'Esmaulx
Conforta, ce dit l'Euvangille,
Me monstra une bonne ville
Et pourveue du don d'esperance :
Combien que pechiez si soit ville,
Rien ne het que perseverance.

14   Je suis pecheur, je le sçay bien ;
Pourtant ne veult pas Dieu ma mort,
Mais convertisse et vive en bien,
Et tout autre que pechié mort.
Combien qu'en pechié soye mort.
Dieu vit, et sa misericorde,
Se conscïence me remort,
Par sa grace pardon m'acorde.

15   Et comme le noble *Roumant
De la Rose* dit et confesse
En son premier commancement
Qu'on doit jeune cueur en jeunesse,
Quant on le voit viel en viellesse,
Excuser, helas ! il dit voir.
Ceulx donc qui me font telle presse
En meureté ne me vouldroient voir.

16   Se pour ma mort le bien publicque
D'aucune chose vaulsist mieulx,
A mourir comme ung homme inique
Je me jugasse, ainsi m'est Dieu !
Griefz ne faiz à jeunes ne vieux,
Soie sur piez ou soye en bierre :
Les mons ne bougent de leurs lieux
Pour ung povre, n'avant, n'arriere.

13　And yet, when I could fare no worse,
　　Being stony-broke on stony ways,
　　God, who consoled at Emmaus
　　Those pilgrims, as the Gospel says,　　　　100
　　Showed me a goodly city,* whose
　　Gift was the hope I might be blest.
　　However wicked sinning is,
　　It's stubborn sin that God detests.

14　Though I'm a sinner, God above
　　Seeks not my death, but wills that I
　　Should turn from wickedness and live,
　　With others whom sin eats away.
　　For even though in sin I die,
　　God's mercy lives; and if remorse　　　　110
　　Of conscience gnaws me, surely He
　　Shall grant me pardon by His grace.

15　And as the *Romance of the Rose*,
　　That noble book, declares in rhyme
　　Right at the start: a man who sees
　　How a young heart that's in its prime
　　Grows old and faint, alas, with time,
　　Must then excuse it – thus the sage.
　　It's why the dogs who hunt me down
　　Would hate to see me in old age.　　　　120

16　If my death served the public good,
　　I'd suffer by my own decree
　　A felon's death, God knows I would!
　　But I have done no injury
　　To old or young that I can see,
　　Whether above or under earth.
　　A poor man's deeds, take it from me,
　　Don't move the mountains back and forth.

17   Ou temps qu'Alixandre regna,
Ungs homs nommé Dïomedés
Devant lui on lui admena
Engrillonné pousses et detz
Comme larron, car il fut des
Escumeurs que voyons courir ;
Sy fut mis devant ce cadés
Pour estre jugiez à mourir.

18   L'empereur si l'araisonna :
« Pourquoi es tu laron en mer ? »
L'autre responce lui donna :
« Pourquoy laron me faiz clamer ?
Pour ce qu'on me voit escumer
En une petïote fuste ?
Se comme toy me peusse armer,
Comme toy empereur je feusse.

19   « Mais que veulx tu ! De ma fortune,
Contre qui ne puis bonnement,
Qui se faulcement me fortune,
Me vient tout ce gouvernement.
Excusez moy aucunement
Et saichiez qu'en grant povreté,
(Ce mot se dit communement)
Ne gist pas grande loyaulté. »

20   Quant l'empereur ot remiré
De Dïomedés tout le dit,
« Ta fortune je te mueray
Mauvaise en bonne », ce lui dist.
Si fist il. Onc puis ne mesdit
A personne, mais fut vray homme.
Valere pour vray le bauldit,
Qui fut nommé le Grant à Romme.

17   In days when Alexander reigned,
      They brought before him to be tried   130
      A man called Diomedes, chained
      And with a thumbscrew surely tied
      As is a thief, for he roved wide
      With other pirates on the seas;
      Now, faced by death, he must abide
      The sentence this great chief decrees.

18   The Emperor accused him: "Why
      Are you a pirate on the sea?"
      To which the other made reply:
      "Why put this pirate name on me?   140
      Is it because I comb the seas
      With one small skiff, and that must do?
      If I could have your armoury,
      I'd be an emperor like you.

19   "But there it is, the work of chance,
      Against whose force I'm powerless,
      She plays me false and brings mischance,
      And that is why I'm in this mess.
      You ought to pity my distress:
      And know that in great poverty   150
      (This is a proverb, more or less)
      There lies but little loyalty."

20   The Emperor paused to reflect
      On all that Diomedes said.
      "I'll change that chance and its effect
      From bad to good" – that's what he said.
      And so he did. Our Diomed
      Left off his slander and became
      An honest man, or so I read
      In great Valerius of Rome.   160

21   Se Dieu m'eust donné rencontrer
    Ung autre piteux Alixandre
    Qui m'eust fait en bon eur entrer,
    Et lors, qui m'eust veu condescendre
    A mal, estre ars et mis en cendre
    Jugié me feusse de ma voys.
    Neccessité fait gens mesprendre
    Et fain saillir le loup du boys.

22   Je plains le temps de ma jeunesse
    Ouquel j'ay plus qu'autre gallé
    Jusqu'à l'entrée de viellesse,
    Qui son partement m'a cellé ;
    Il ne s'en est à pié alé
    N'à cheval : helas ! comment don ?
    Soudainement s'en est vollé
    Et ne m'a laissié quelque don.

23   Alé s'en est, et je demeure,
    Povre de sens et de savoir,
    Triste, failly, plus noir que meure,
    Qui n'ay de cens, rente, n'avoir.
    Des miens le mendre, je dy voir,
    De me desavouer s'avance,
    Oubliant naturel devoir
    Par faulte d'un peu de chevance.

24   Si ne crains avoir despendu
    Par friander ne par lescher ;
    Par trop amer n'ay rien vendu
    Que nulz me puisse reprouchier,
    Au moins qui leur couste moult cher.
    Je le dy, et ne croys mesdire.
    De ce je me puis revanchier :
    Qui n'a meffait ne le doit dire.

21   If God had given me the luck
      To meet some pitying Alexander
      And find through him a better track,
      My own poor body I would render
      And let them burn it to a cinder,
      If then I turned away from good.
      It's need that fosters crime, and hunger
      That brings the wolf out of the wood.

22   I mourn my youthful season, when
      Far more than most I had my fling   170
      Until old age came knocking; then
      Youth left, but hid its leave-taking,
      Not walking out or galloping:
      How did it go then? Fast and free
      It rose and suddenly took wing,
      And left no parting gift for me.

23   Well, gone it is, and I remain,
      Poor both in knowledge and in sense,
      Black as a mulberry, in pain,
      And with no income, goods or rents: 180
      I swear my poorest cousin's bent
      On showing he disowns me, and
      Denies what nature would consent
      Because I have no cash in hand.

24   No, I don't think I've spent above
      My share on feasts and gluttony.
      And nothing that I sold for love
      Would justify men blaming me:
      Mine was a low-cost lechery!
      I know that I'm not wrong on this.   190
      I can defend myself, for he
      Who hasn't sinned should not confess.

25   Bien est verté que j'é aymé
      Et aymeroye voulentiers,
      Mais triste cueur, ventre affamé,
      Qui n'est rassasïé au tiers,
      M'oste des amoureux sentiers.
      Au fort, quelc'um s'en recompence
      Qui est remply sur les chantiers,
      Car de la pance vient la dance.

26   Bien sçay, se j'eusse estudïé
      Ou temps de ma jeunesse folle
      Et à bonnes meurs dedïé,
      J'eusse maison et couche molle.
      Mais quoy ! je fuyoie l'escolle
      Comme fait le mauvaiz enffant.
      En escripvant ceste parolle,
      A peu que le cueur ne me fent.

27   Le dit du Saige trop lui feiz
      Favorable (bien en puis mais !)
      Qui dist : « Esjoïs toy, mon filz,
      En ton adolessence », mes
      Ailleurs sert bien d'un autre mes,
      Car « Jeunesse et adolessance »
      (C'est son parler, ne moins ne mes)
      « Ne sont qu'abuz et ygnorance ».

28   Mes jours s'en sont alez errant
      Comme, dit Job, d'une touaille
      Font les filletz, quant tixerant
      En son poing tient ardente paille :
      Lors, s'il y a nul bout qui saille,
      Soudainement il le ravit.
      Sy ne crains riens que plus m'assaille,
      Car à la mort tout s'assouvit.

38

25 Yes, I have loved, that's true enough,
    And would again with right good will,
    But there are things that put me off:
    My sad heart and a gut that still
    Has two thirds of its space to fill.
    Time to give someone else a chance,
    Some tub of guts will fit the bill,
    For it's the belly leads the dance.   200

26 My youth was wild, and this I know:
    If I had stuck to books instead,
    If I'd behaved myself, by now
    I'd have a house and a soft bed.
    Fat chance! Not me, I skived and fled
    The school as bad boys always do.
    Writing those words I feel as sad
    As if my heart would break in two.

27 I trusted too much in the truth
    Of the old Sage* (much good it's done!)   210
    When he said, "In your days of youth
    Rejoice, enjoy yourself, my son."
    But then he sings a different tune –
    I give the text for you to see,
    (No more, no less, as written down):
    "Childhood and youth are vanity".*

28 My days have vanished like the ends
    Of thread the weaver sets aflame
    With a straw burning in his hand
    When they protrude beyond the frame,   220
    So Job says* – and I feel the same:
    Gone in a flash, as he attests.
    And so I fear not what may come,
    For death brings all things down to rest.

39

29   Où sont les gracïeux galants
       Que je suivoye ou temps jadiz,
       Si bien chantans, si bien parlans,
       Sy plaisans en faiz et en diz ?
       Les aucuns sont mors et roidiz,
       D'eulx n'est il plus riens maintenant ;
       Respit ilz aient en paradis,
       Et Dieu saulve le remenant !

30   Et les autres sont devenuz
       Dieu mercy, grans seigneurs et maistres ;
       Les autres mendient tous nuz
       Et pain ne voient qu'aux fenestres.
       Les autres sont entrez es cloistres
       De Celestins et de Chartreux,
       Bostés, houlsés com pescheurs d'oestres.
       Voyez l'estat divers d'entr'eux !

31   Aux grans maistres Dieu doint bien fere,
       Vivans en paix et en requoy ;
       En eulx il n'y a que reffaire :
       Si s'en fait bon taire tout quoy.
       Mais aux povres qui n'ont de quoy,
       Comme moy, Dieu doint pascience !
       Aux autres ne fault qui ne quoy,
       Car assez ont pain et pictence.

32   Bons vins ont, souvent embrochez,
       Saulces, brouestz et groz poissons,
       Tartes, flans, oefz fritz et pochetz,
       Perduz et en toutes façons.
       Pas ne ressemblent les maçons,
       Que servir fault à si grant peine ;
       Ilz ne veullent nulz eschançons :
       De soy verser chacun se paine.

29   Where are they now, the lads I hung
      Around with once, a dashing breed,
      Fine in their speech, fine in their song,
      Charming in every word and deed?
      Now some of them are stiff and dead,
      They left no traces; may they find   230
      Pardon in Paradise, and God
      Save all those who are left behind!

30   And some of these have been well fed,
      Thank God, they're now great lords and masters;
      Some, naked, get their daily bread
      As window-shoppers, not as tasters.
      Others have made their way to cloisters,
      Carthusians or Celestines,
      Booted like men who fish for oysters:
      What various fortunes fate assigns!   240

31   God grant that masters may do good,
      Living in quiet and in peace,
      There's nothing in them that I should
      Change, so I'd better hold my peace;
      But may God's gift of patience bless
      The down and out like me, the poor.
      The needs of monks should count much less:
      They have their bread and butter sure.

32   Good wines they have, not seldom broached,
      Fat fish and stews, all kinds of sauce,   250
      Pastries and pies, eggs fried and poached
      Or cooked to go with any course.
      They're not like stonemasons who force
      Apprentices to pour their wine;
      Waiters aren't wanted there because
      They think self-service suits them fine.

33   En cest incident me suis mis
      Qui de rien ne sert à mon fait.
      Je ne suis juge ne commis
      Pour pugnir n'assouldre meffait :
      De tout suis le plus imparfait,
      Loué soit le doulx Jhesu Crist !
      Que par moy leur soy satisfait.
      Ce que j'ay escript est escript.

34   Laissons le moustier où il est :
      Parlons de chose plus plaisante ;
      Ceste matiere à tous ne plest,
      Ennuieuse est et desplaisante.
      Povreté, chagrine, doulente,
      Tousjours, despiteuse et rebelle,
      Dit quelque parolle cuisante ;
      Si elle n'ose, si le pense elle.

35   Povre je suis de ma jeunesse,
      De povre et de peticte extrasse,
      Mon pere n'eust oncq grant richesse,
      Ne son ayeul, nommé Orrace ;
      Povreté tous nous suit et trace.
      Sur les tumbeaux de mes ancestres
      (Les ames desquelz Dieu embrasse !)
      On n'y voit couronnes ne ceptres.

36   De povreté me grementant,
      Souventeffoiz me dit le cueur :
      « Homme, ne te doulouse tant
      Et ne demaine tel douleur.
      Se tu n'as tant qu'eust Jaques Cueur,
      Mieulx vault vivre soubz gros bureau
      Pouvre, qu'avoir esté seigneur
      Et pourrir soubz riche tumbeau. »

33   While I allow myself to prate
      My theme gets lost and I digress.
      I'm neither judge nor magistrate
      To censure others who transgress.   260
      All praise to Jesus! I confess
      I have most need to be forgiven.
      Let my amends by made by this.
      What I have written I have written.*

34   Let's leave the abbey where it is
      And speak of something that's more jolly;
      Not all men love a theme like this:
      It's grim, offensive, melancholy.
      For Poverty that's sad and surly
      Speaks in a bitter cutting way,   270
      And if she's ever dumb, then surely
      She thinks the things she dare not say.

35   Poor I have been from childhood on,
      Born of a poor and lowly race;
      Grandfather Horace and his son
      Met no great riches on their ways;
      Poverty marks us with its trace.
      Upon the tombs of my ancestors
      (God clasp their souls in His embrace!)
      You won't find any crowns and sceptres.   280

36   When I complain of being poor,
      My heart repeats time and again:
      "Look, man, no need to feel so sore
      And go about as if in pain.
      Rich as Jacques Cœur you're not; but then
      Better to live, so I assume,
      In homespun cloth than to have been
      A lord and rot in a rich tomb."

43

37   Qu'avoir esté seigneur... Que dis ?
       Seigneur, lasse ! ne l'est il mais ?
       Selon ce que David en dist,
       Son lieu ne congnoistra jamaiz.
       Quant du seurplus je m'en desmez :
       Il n'appartient à moy, pecheur ;
       Aux theologiens le remectz,
       Car c'est office de prescheur.

38   Sy ne suis, bien le considere,
       Filz d'ange portant diadame
       D'estoille ne d'autre sidere.
       Mon pere est mort : Dieu en ait l'ame !
       Quant est du corps, il gist soubz lame.
       J'entens que ma mere mourra
       (El le scet bien, la povre femme)
       Et le filz pas ne demourra.

39   Je congnois que pouvres et riches,
       Sagez et folz, prestres et laiz,
       Nobles, villains, larges et chiches,
       Petiz et grans, et beaulx et laitz,
       Dames à rebrassés colletz
       De quelconque condicïon,
       Portans atours et bourreletz,
       Mort saisit sans excepcïon.

40   Et meure Paris ou Elayne,
       Quicunques meurt, meurt à douleur :
       Cellui qui pert vent et alaine,
       Son fiel se criefve sur son cueur,
       Puis sue Dieu scet quel sueur !
       Et qui de ses maulx si l'alège ?
       Car enffant n'a, frere ne seur,
       Qui lors voulsist estre son pleige.

37   "To have been a lord"… You mean to say
       He's not the lord he was before?   290
       Alas, let's put it David's way:
       His place shall know of him no more.*
       As for the rest, I must demur;
       Sinners like me should not aspire:
       To theologians I defer,
       The job best suits a preaching friar.

38   Of course, I see I'm very far
       From being an angel's son with crown
       That bears a comet or a star:
       God make my father's soul his own!   300
       His body lies beneath a stone.
       Mother will die, I understand
       (Poor thing, she knows it) and her son
       Won't linger very long behind.

39   The poor and rich I call to mind,
       The priest and layman, sage and fool,
       Noble and peasant, mean or kind,
       The fair and ugly, great and small,
       Ladies whose plunging necklines fall
       Too low (whatever their estate),   310
       While headgear makes them very tall –
       Death seizes them, leaves no one out.

40   Paris and Helen meet their death:
       So what! Whoever dies, it hurts:
       He has no wind and fights for breath
       As the bile bursts and floods the heart:
       And then he sweats, God knows what sweat!
       No one relieves his pain and fears:
       Would brother, sister, play the part
       Of stand-in? Strange! No volunteers.   320

41   La mort le fait fremir, pallir,
          Le nez courber, les vaines tendre,
          Le col enffler, la chair moslir,
          Joinctes et nerfz croistre et estendre.
          Corps femenin, qui tant est tendre,
          Poly, souëf, si precïeulx,
          Te fauldra il ces maulx attendre ?
          Oy — ou tout vif aler es cieulx.

Ballade des dames du temps jadis

      Dictes moy où, n'en quel pays,
      Est Flora, la belle Romaine,
      Archipiadès ne Thaÿs,
      Qui fut sa cousine germaine,
      Echo parlant quant bruyt on maine
      Dessus riviere ou sur estan,
      Qui beaulté ot trop plus qu'umaine.
      Mais où sont les neiges d'anten ?

      Où est la tressaige Esloÿs,
      Pour qui chastré fut et puis moyne
      Pierre Esbaillart à Saint Denys ?
      Pour son amour eust ceste essoyne !
      Semblablement, où est la royne
      Qui commanda que Buriden
      Fut gecté en ung sac en Saine ?
      Mais où sont les neiges d'anten ?

      La Royne Blanche comme liz,
      Qui chantoit à voix de seraine,
      Berte au plat pié, Bietrix, Aliz,
      Haranburgis qui tint le Maine,
      Et Jehanne, la bonne Lorraine,
      Qu'Engloys brulerent à Rouen,
      Où sont ilz, où, Vierge souveraine ?
      Mais où sont les neiges d'anten ?

Death makes him tremble and turn pale,
His nose grows curved, his veins protrude,
His neck swells up, his flesh grows frail,
His joints and sinews stretch and spread.
And woman's body, so imbued
With smooth and soft, so highly prized,
Must you expect these ills? Indeed,
Or rise alive to Paradise.

Ballade of the Ladies of Times Past*

Say where, in what far country is
Flora, the splendid Roman lass,   330
Archipiada or Thaïs,
Whose kindred beauty was no less,
Echo, respeaking sounds that pass
Over swift stream or stagnant mere,
Who outshone human loveliness?
But where are the snows that fell last year?

Where now is learned Héloïse,
Whose love brought Abelard disgrace,
Castrated, then at Saint-Denis
Condemned to be a monk at last?   340
And where's that queen whose high behest
Said Buridan should disappear
(Thrown bagged into the Seine he was)?
But where are the snows that fell last year?

Queen Blanche, more white than lily is,
Who sang with such a siren voice,
Flat-footed Bertha, Beatrice,
Alice and Arembourg (Maine's her place),
Brave Joan of Lorraine whom the base
English at Rouen burned in fear,   350
Where are they, Virgin full of grace?
But where are the snows that fell last year?

Prince, n'enquerrez de sepmaine
Où elles sont, ne de cest an,
Qu'à ce reffraing ne vous remaine :
Mais où sont les neiges d'anten ?

Ballade des seigneurs du temps jadis

Qui plus, où est ly tiers Calixte,
Dernier decedé de ce nom,
Quy quatre ans tint le papalixte,
Alfonce le roy d'Arragon,
Le graciëux duc de Bourbon,
Et Artus le duc de Bretaigne,
Et Charles septiesme le bon ?
Mais où est le preux Charlemaigne ?

Semblablement , le roy Scotiste
Qui demy face ot, ce dit on,
Vermaille comme une emastiste
Depuis le front jusq'au menton,
Le roy de Chippre de renom,
Helas ! et le bon roy d'Espaigne
Duquel je ne sçay pas le nom ?
Mais où est le preux Charlemaigne ?

D'en plus parler je me desiste :
Le monde n'est qu'abusïon.
Il n'est qui contre mort resiste
Ne qui treuve provisïon.
Encore faiz une questïon :
Lancellot, le roy de Behaygne
Où est il ? où est son tayon ?
Mais où est le preux Charlemaigne ?

Où est Clacquin, le bon Breton ?
Où le comte Daulphin d'Auvergne,

Prince, let a week, a twelvemonth pass,
And do not ask where now they are,
Lest my refrain be yours at last:
But where are the snows that fell last year?

Ballade of the Lords of Times Past

What's more, where's Calixtus the Third,
Last of that name, now dead and gone,
Pope for four years or so I've heard,
Alfonso, king of Aragon,   360
And then the handsome Duke Bourbon,
The seventh Charles who used to reign
And old Duke Arthur the Breton?
But where's the worthy Charlemagne?

The Scots king, half whose face was marred
By a great mark, they say, that shone
Red as an amethyst and scarred
Him all the way from brow to chin;
The Cypriot king of great renown,
Alas, and the good king of Spain   370
(I knew his name once, now it's gone)?
But where's the worthy Charlemagne?

There's nothing more I mean to add;
The world's a cheat. There is no one
Can stave off death or plan ahead
Against its mortal coming on.
Just one last question, then I'm done:
That Lancelot who used to reign
In far Bohemia, where's he gone?
But where's the worthy Charlemagne?   380

Where is Guesclin, the good Breton?
Or the count Dauphin of Auvergne?

Et le bon feu duc d'Alençon ?
Mais où est le preux Charlemaigne ?

Ballade

Car, ou soit ly sains appostolles,
D'aubes vestuz, d'amys coeffez,
Qui ne seint fors saintes estolles,
Dont par le col prent ly mauffez
De mal talant tous eschauffez,
Aussi bien meurt que cilz servans,
De ceste vie cy buffez :
Autant en emporte ly vens.

Voire, ou soit de Constantinobles
L'emperieures au poing dorez,
Ou de France le roy tresnobles,
Sur tous autres roys decorez,
Qui pour ly grant Dieux adorez
Batist esglises et couvens,
S'en son temps il fut honnorez,
Autant en emporte ly vens.

Ou soit de Vïenne et Grenobles
Ly Daulphin, le preux, ly senez,
Ou de Digons, Salins et Dolles
Ly sires, filz le plus esnez,
Ou autant de leurs gens prenez :
Heraux, trompectes, poursuivans ;
Ont ilz bien boutez soubz le nez ?
Autant en emporte ly vens.

Prince, à mort sont tous destinez
Et tous autres qui sont vivans ;
S'ilz en sont courcez n'atinez,
Autant en emporte ly vens.

The late brave duke of Alençon?
But where's the worthy Charlemagne?

Ballade

For whether it's His Holiness
With alb and amice on his back,
With holy stole to gird his dress
And catch that Devil by the neck
Who flames with lust to cause our wreck,
Like some poor groom, he too will die,   390
Puffed into nothing, merely smoke:
The wind still bears it all away.

Or else the Emperor whose gold fist
Constantinople grieves to lack,
The noble King of France, the first
Among all other kings – whose work
Built abbey, chapel, convent, kirk,
For love of God – if, in his day,
He gained high honour's every mark,
The wind still bears it all away.   400

Grenoble and Vienne are blest
For their wise Dauphin's valiant sake,
And Dijon, Salins, Dole profess
Great sires and the heirs they make;
What of their people? Shall we take
Heralds and henchmen, horns that bray,
Stuffed up until their bellies ache?
The wind still bears it all away.

Prince, death's the destiny that makes
An end to all, all go that way;   410
Who cares how much offence they take?
The wind still bears it all away.

42   Puis que pappes, roys, filz de roys
      Et conceuz en ventre de roynes
      Sont enseveliz mors et froys
      (En aultruy mains passent leur regnes),
      Moy, povre marcerot de regnes,
      Morrai ge pas ? Oy, se Dieu plaist ;
      Mais que j'ay fait mes estraines,
      Honneste mort ne me desplaist.

43   Ce monde n'est perpetuel,
      Quoy que pense riche pillart.
      Tous sommes soubz mortel coustel :
      Ce confort prent povre viellart,
      Lequel d'estre plaisant raillart
      Ot le bruyt, lors que jeune estoit,
      C'on tiendroit à fol et paillart
      Se, viel, à raillier se mestoit.

44   Car s'en jeunesse il fut plaisant,
      Ores plus riens ne dit qui plaise.
      Tousjours viel singe est desplaisant ;
      Moue ne fait qui ne desplaise.
      S'il se taist, affin qu'il complaise.
      Il est tenu pour fol recreu ;
      S'il parle, on luy dist qu'il se taise
      Et qu'en son prunier n'a pas creu.

45   Or lui convient il mendïer,
      Car ad ce force le contrainct.
      Regrecte huy sa mort et hier :
      Tristesse son cueur si estaint :
      Se, souvent, n'estoit Dieu qu'il craint,
      Il feroit ung orrible fait,
      Et advient qu'en ce Dieu enffraint
      Et que lui mesme se deffait.

42   Since popes and kings and princes bold,
        Conceived in royal wombs, must lie
        Beneath the gravestone, dead and cold,
        While others rule instead, shall I,
        Poor pedlar selling words, not die?
        Well yes, if that's what God intends;
        Just let me have my piece of pie,
        I'll settle for an honest end.   420

43   This world can't last for ever, though
        The thieving rich may think it can.
        A sword hangs over us: and so
        Let that console some poor old man
        Who, in his youth, was hailed as crown
        And soul of wit each time he spoke;
        Now, he'd be called a senile clown
        If he so much as cracked a joke.

44   Men shared the joke when he was young,
        Now nothing that he says finds grace.   430
        An old ape always gets it wrong:
        Nobody smiles at his grimace.
        Silence won't help in such a case,
        They'll say that he's decrepit, dumb;
        Speak then – he's told to shut his face,
        For his old fruit is no fresh plum.

45   And now in his necessity
        Begging becomes his last resort.
        Day after day he longs to die,
        Sorrow so clutches at his heart: 440
        But for the fear that stops him short
        He'd do the awful deed that would
        Break the stern law that God has taught,
        And thus destroy himself for good.

53

46   Aussi ces povres famelettes
       Qui vielles sont, et n'ont de quoy,
       Quant ilz voient ces pucellettes
       Empruncter elles à requoy,
       Ilz demandent à Dieu pourquoy
       Sy tost nacquirent, n'à quel droit.
       Nostre Seigneur se taist tout quoy,
       Car au tancer il le perdroit.

Les Regrets de la belle Heaulmière

47   Advis m'est que j'oy regrecter
       La belle qui fut Hëaulmiere,
       Soy jeune fille soubzhaicter
       Et parler en telle maniere :
       « A ! Viellesse felonne et fiere,
       Pourquoy m'as si tost abatue ?
       Qui me tient, qui, que ne me fiere
       Et qu'à ce coup je ne me tue ?

48   « Tollu m'as la haulte franchise
       Que Beaulté m'avoit ordonné
       Sur clers, marchans et gens d'Eglise,
       Car lors il n'estoit homme né
       Que tout le scien ne m'eust donné,
       Quoy qu'il en feust de repentailles,
       Mais que lui eusse abandonné
       Ce que reffusent truandailles.

49   « A maint homme l'ay reffusé,
       Qui n'estoit à moy grant sagesse,
       Pour l'amour d'un garson rusé,
       Auquel j'en feiz grande largesse.
       A qui que je feisse fynesse,
       Par m'ame je l'aymoye bien.
       Or ne me faisoit que rudesse
       Et ne m'aimoit que pour le mien.

46   With poor old women it's the same,
For when their source of cash runs dry,
And when young chicks go on the game
To nick their clients on the sly,
They turn to God and ask him why
He had them born so prematurely.   450
Our Lord says nothing; should He try
A war of words, He'd lose it surely.

The Complaint of the Fair Armouress*

47   I seem to hear a voice complain:
Once called the Lovely Armouress,
She longs to be a girl again
And speaks as follows, more or less:
"Ah, cruel Age, you foul traitress,
Why beat me down so soon, so low?
Who stops me, who, from ending this?
I'd do it with a single blow.   460

48   "You've robbed me of what was my due,
The power I held, as Beauty planned,
Over clerks, merchants, clergy too;
For no man born in all the land
Would not have sold up out of hand
(Leaving remorse for retrospect),
If only he could get his hand
On what the rabble now reject.

49   "I told so many men hands off
(This doesn't say much for my wit)   470
Because I loved a sly young toff
And gave him the free run of it.
I might lead others on a bit,
But, by my soul, I loved him fine!
He went on messing me about
And loved me just for what was mine.

50   « Sy ne me sceust tant detrainer,
       Fouller aux piez, que ne l'aymasse,
       Et m'eust il fait les rains trayner,
       S'il m'eust dit que je le baisasse,
       Que tous mes maulx je n'oubliasse.
       Le glouton, de mal entaichié,
       M'embrassoit… J'en suis bien plus grasse !
       Que m'en rest'il ? Honte et pechié.

51   « Or est il mort, passé trente ans,
       Et je remains, vielle, chenue.
       Quant je pense, lasse, au bon temps,
       Que me regarde toute nue
       (Quelle fuz, quelle devenue !)
       Et je me voy si treschangée,
       Povre, seiche, maigre, menue,
       Je suis presque toute enraigée.

52   « Qu'est devenu ce front poly,
       Cheveux blons, ces sourciz voultiz,
       Grant entreuil, ce regard joly
       Dont prenoië les plus soubtilz,
       Ce beau nez droit, grant ne petiz,
       Ces petites joinctes orreilles,
       Menton fourchu, cler viz traictiz,
       Et ces belles levres vermeilles ?

53   « Ces gentes espaulles menues,
       Ces bras longs et ces mains traictisses,
       Petiz tetins, hanches charnues,
       Eslevées, propres et faictisses
       A tenir amoureuses lices,
       Ces larges reins, ce sadinet
       Assiz sur grosses fermes cuisses
       Dedans son petit jardinet ?

50   "He could have knocked me on the track
        And trampled me; I loved him still.
        And if he'd dragged me on my back,
        One kiss would be enough to heal   480
        Those wounds that I'd forget to feel.
        For when the deep-died scoundrel came
        And took me in his arms… Big deal!
        What's left me now? The sin and shame.

51   "He's dead these thirty years, and I
        Remain behind, grown grey with care.
        I think on the good times gone by,
        And when I see myself stripped bare
        (My body then and now – compare!)
        And find how I have changed with age,
        Dried up and skinny, poor and spare,   490
        I think that I shall burst with rage.

52   "Where's the smooth forehead I had once,
        The arching eyebrows, the blond hair,
        The wide-set eyes, the playful glance
        That caught the wariest in its snare,
        The ears, a lovely dainty pair,
        The straight nose, neither big nor small,
        The dimpled chin, face clear and fair,
        And full red lips to crown it all?   500

53   "Those lovely shoulders, slim and slight,
        Long arms, hands slender and refined,
        Those small high breasts, those hips just right,
        Solid and supple, well designed
        For contact sports (the amorous kind);
        The good wide loins, the little grot
        Surmounting sturdy thighs, enshrined
        Within its shady garden plot?

54 « Le front ridé, les cheveux griz,
Les sourciz cheux, les yeulx estains,
Qui faisoient regars et ris
Dont maints meschans furent actains,
Nez courbes, de beaulté loingtaings,
Orreilles pendentes, moussues,
Le visz paly, mort et destains,
Menton froncé, levres peaussues...

55 « C'est d'umaine beaulté l'yssue !
Les braz cours et les mains contraictes,
Des espaulles toute bossue,
Mamelles, quoy ? toutes retraictes :
Telles les hanches que les tectes.
Du sadinet ? Fy ! Quant des cuisses,
Cuisses ne sont plus, mais cuissectes
Grivelées comme saulcisses.

56 « Ainsi le bon temps regretons
Entre nous, povres vielles soctes,
Assises bas, à crouppetons,
Tout en ung tas, comme peloctes,
A petit feu de chenevoctes,
Tost aluméës, tost estainctes...
Et jadiz fusmes si mignotes !
Ainsi en prent à maint et maintes. »

Ballade de la belle Heaulmiere aux filles de joie

« Or y pensez, belle Gantiere,
Qui escolliere souliez estre,
Et vous, Blanche la Savetiere :
Ores est temps de vous congnoistre :
Prenez à destre et à senestre,
N'espargniez homme, je vous prie,
Car vielles n'ont ne cours ne estre
Ne que monnoye qu'on descrye.

54   "Forehead all wrinkled, hair turned grey,
      Eyebrows collapsed and bleary eyes –   510
      Those eyes that once shone bright and gay
      And caught their victims by surprise;
      Hooked nose (that's not where beauty lies),
      Hairs on the pendulous ears and chin,
      A pallid face where colour dies,
      A puckered mouth, and lips mere skin…

55   "This is how human beauty ends!
      Shoulders hunched-up and all askew,
      Contracted arms and clawlike hands,
      Breasts shrivelled, hips gone that way too.   520
      As for the little grotto – Phoo!
      Don't ask about the thighs, they're not
      Thighs any longer, more like two
      Leftover sausages with spots.

56   "So we regret the good times gone,
      Chatting among ourselves like fools,
      Old biddies squatting down upon
      The ground, bunched up like woollen balls,
      By the hemp-stick fire growing cool,
      Soon lit and soon put out again…   530
      To think we were such lovely girls!
      That's how it goes with women, and men."

Ballade of the Fair Armouress to the Girls on the Game

      "Think of it, lovely Glover Girl,*
      My novice not so long ago,
      And Blanche the Cobbler (such a pearl!),
      It's time you heard what you should know:
      Take right and left, but never show
      Any man mercy, don't be tender;
      Old women rate about as low
      As coins that are not legal tender.   540

« Et vous, la gente Saulcissiere,
Qui de dancer estes adestre,
Guillemete la Tappiciere,
Ne mesprenez vers vostre maistre !
Tost vous fauldra clore fenestre :
Quant deviendrez vielle, flestrye,
Plus ne servirez q'un viel prestre
Ne que monnoye c'on descrye.

« Jehanneton la Chapperonniere,
Gardez qu'amy ne vous empestre,
Et Katherine la Bourciere,
N'envoyer plus les hommes paistre.
Car, qui belle n'est, ne perpestre
Leur malgrace, mais leur rie :
Laide viellesse amour n'impestre
Ne que monnoye c'on descrye.

« Filles, vueillez vous entremectre
D'escouter pourquoy pleure et crye :
Pource que je ne me puis mectre
Ne que monnoye c'on descrye. »

57   Ceste leçon icy leur baille
La belle et bonne de jadiz.
Bien dit ou mal, vaille que vaille,
Enregistrer j'ay fait ses diz
Par mon clerc Fremin l'Estourdiz,
Aussi rassiz que je pense estre.
S'il me desment, je le mauldiz :
Selon le clerc est deu le maistre.

"And you, good Sausage-Girl, who pass
For deft at dancing to and fro,
And Guillemette, the Carpet-Lass,
Respect your teacher! Soon, your show
Will have to close because you'll grow
Wrinkled and old, not smooth and slender.
Then some old priest will have to do:
Your coin will not be legal tender.

"Jane Bonneteer, don't let your course
Be hampered by your latest beau,   550
And Kate, best maker of a purse,
Don't warn men off: plain girls, you know,
Can stay in favour if they show
No spite, but smiles and sweet surrender:
Love shuns the old and ugly, so
Their coin's no longer legal tender.

"Girls, listen to my tale of woe,
These cries that rend the air asunder:
I'm out of circulation now,
Because my coin's not legal tender."   560

57   This is the lesson that they heard
     Delivered by the ruined belle;
     Well said or no, I've had her words,
     For what they're worth, transcribed in full
     By Dumb Fremin,* my clerk, who well
     May be as smart as me, I own.
     If he says not, I'll give him hell,
     For by the clerk the master's known.

58   Sy apperçoy le grant danger
        Ouquel l'omme amoureux se boute.
        Et qui me vouldroit laidanger
        De ce mot, en disant. « Escoute !
        Se d'amer t'estrange et reboute
        Le barrat de celles nommées,
        Tu faiz une bien folle doubte,
        Car ce sont femmes diffamées.

59   « S'ilz n'ayment fors que pour l'argent,
        On ne les ayme que pour l'eure.
        Rondement ayment toute gent
        Et rient lors quant bourse pleure ;
        De celles cy n'est qui ne queurre.
        Mais en femmes d'onneur et nom
        Franc homme, se Dieu me sequeure,
        Se doit emploier, ailleurs non. »

60   Je prens qu'aucun dye cecy,
        Sy ne me contente il en rien.
        En effect, il conclud ainsi,
        (Et je le cuide entendre bien)
        Qu'on doit amer en lieu de bien.
        Assavoir mon se ces fillectes
        Qu'en parolles toute jour tien,
        Ne furent ilz femmes honnestes ?

61   Honnestes si furent vrayement,
        Sans avoir reprouches ne blasmes.
        Sy est vray qu'au commencement
        Une chascune de ces femmes
        Lors prindrent, ains qu'eussent diffames,
        L'une ung clerc, ung lay, l'autre ung moyne,
        Pour estaindre d'amour leurs flasmes
        Plus chaudes que feu saint Anthoyne.

58   From what's been said the frightful risk
      A man in love must run is clear.   570
      So someone then takes me to task
      For these harsh words with: "Listen here!
      If you are scared by love for fear
      Of dirty deals from those we've named,
      It really isn't all that queer,
      Because such women are ill-famed.

59   "If money's all they love, so men
      Love them but for the hour that flies.
      They grant their love to all, and then
      They laugh to see the purse that cries;   580
      They run wherever there's a prize.
      But honest dames whose name is fair,
      That's where a good man turns his eyes,
      And not – God help us! – not elsewhere."

60   I take it that's what people say,
      And I don't like it, not one bit.
      The fact is he concludes this way
      (I think I've got the gist of it):
      That only honest girls are fit
      For us to love. But don't you know?   590
      These girls I chat with, let's admit,
      Were honest too not long ago?

61   Honest they were, without a doubt,
      And free from all reproach and blame.
      I speak of when they started out,
      Before they ruined their good name.
      Each of them took, just as he came,
      A clerk, a layman, monk or friar
      To quench the burning of love's flame
      That's hotter than St Anthony's fire.   600

62   Or firent selon ce decret
        Leurs amys, et bien y appert :
        Ilz aimoient en lieu secret,
        Car autre d'eulx n'y avoit part.
        Touteffoiz ceste amour se part,
        Car celle qui n'en avoit q'um
        De celluy s'eslongne et depart,
        Et ayme mieulx aymer chascun.

63   Qui les meut à ce ? G'ymagine
        (Sans l'amour des dames blasmer)
        Que c'est nature femeninne
        Qui tout unyment veult amer.
        Autre chose n'y sçay rimer,
        Fors qu'on dit à Rains et Troys,
        Voire à l'Isle et à Saint Omer,
        Que six ouvriers font plus que trois.

64   Or ont ces folz amans le bont
        Et les dames prins la vollée.
        C'est le droit loier qu'amans ont :
        Toute foy y est vïollée.
        Quelque doulx baisier n'acollée,
        « De chiens, d'oyseaulx, d'armes, d'amours »
        (C'est pure verté devollée)
        « Pour une joye cent doulours. »

Double ballade sur le mesme propos

Pour ce, aymez tant que vouldrez,
Suivez assemblées et festes,
En la fin ja mieulx n'en vauldrez
Et n'y romperez que voz testes.
Folles amours font des gens bestes :
Salmon en ydolatria,
Sanson en perdit ses lunectes.
Bien eureux est qui rien n'y a !

62 According to the rules, they played
    The game discreetly, set apart;
    Exclusively, it must be said,
    For no one else had any part.
    And yet in time the loving heart
    Gets shared, because no girl will fall
    For one man's love, but leave him flat,
    Since she prefers to love them all.

63 What makes them do it? To my mind
    (I mean the ladies no offence)   610
    The female nature is inclined
    To love all men, and all at once.
    On this I'll rhyme no further, since
    At Rheims and Troyes they quite agree
    With Lille and Saint-Omer's good sense:
    Six men can do more work than three.

64 The silly lover is bounced out
    By volleys from his ladylove.
    Such wages are the lovers' lot:
    For all their faith, they'll get the shove.   620
    Those hugs and kisses only prove
    The truth of this well-worn refrain:
    "With dogs and falcons, war and love,
    One pleasure for a thousand pains."

*Double Ballade on the Same Topic**

So go and take your fill of love
With parties, banquets, board and bed,
You'll end up not much better off
And, in the bargain, break your head.
For foolish loving makes men mad:
Idolatry spoiled Solomon's wit,   630
And Samson lost his specs, it's said,
Happy the man who's out of it!

65

Orpheüs, le doulx menestrier,
Jouant de fluctes et musectes,
En fut en danger d'un murtrier
Chien Cerberuz à quatre testes.
Et Narcisus, ly beaulx honnestes,
En ung parfont puis se noya
Pour l'amour de ses amourectes.
Bien eureux est qui rien n'y a !

Sardana, le preux chevallier,
Qui conquist le resne de Crestes,
En voulut devenir moullier
Et filler entre pucellectes.
David ly roys, saiges prophetes,
Crainte de Dieu en oublia,
Voyant laver cuisses bien fetes.
Bien eureux est qui rien n'y a !

Amon en voult deshonnorer,
Faignant de menger tartelectes,
Sa seur Thamar et defflorer,
Qui fut incestes deshonnestes.
Herodes (pas ne sont sornectes)
Saint Jehan Baptiste en decola
Pour dances, saulx et chansonnectes.
Bien eureux est qui rien n'y a !

De moy povre je vueil parler :
J'en fuz batu comme à ru telles,
Tout nu, ja ne le quiers celler.
Qui me fist macher ces groselles
Fors Katherine de Vauselles ?
Noël le tiers ot, qui fut là,
Mitaines à ces nopces telles.
Bien eureux est qui rien n'y a !

And Orpheus with his flute and fife,
Sweet minstrel, went below and played,
And came in danger of his life
From Cerberus with four heads – all bad.
Narcissus, fine upstanding lad,
Found some deep well and thought it fit
To drown himself for love. How sad!
Happy the man who's out of it!   640

Sardana, valiant knight, went off
And conquered Crete; but still he played
A woman's part, and all for love
He took to spinning with the maids.
King David lost the fear of God;
Wise though he was, he could not quit
The sight of well-washed thighs displayed.
Happy the man who's out of it!

Loving his sister, Amnon strove
(Pretending to want tarts instead)   650
To take her virgin honour off
With vile incestuous lust in bed.
A spot of dirty dancing led
Herod (this isn't idle chat)
To cut off John the Baptist's head.
Happy the man who's out of it!

Now for myself: for love my hide
Was like wet laundry beaten flat,*
Stark naked – something I won't hide.
Who made me chew a fruit like that   660
But Kate Vausselles? The third one at
The wedding feast, Noël, got hit
By some good mitts that packed a clout.
Happy the man who's out of it!

Mais que ce jeune bachelier
Laissast ces jeunes bachelectes ?
Non ! Et le deust on vif bruler
Comme ung chevaucheur d'escouvettes.
Plus doulces lui sont que cyvetes,
Mais touteffoiz fol s'i fya :
Soient blanches, soient brunectes,
Bien eureux est qui rien n'y a !

65   Se celle que jadiz servoye
       De si bon cueur et loyaulment,
       Dont tant de maulx et griefz j'avoye
       Et souffroye tant de tourment,
       Se dit m'eust, au commancement,
       Sa voulenté (mais nennil, las !)
       J'eusse mis paine aucunement
       De moy retraire de ses las.

66   Quoy que je lui voulsisse dire,
       Elle estoit preste d'escouter
       Sans m'acorder ne contredire.
       Qui plus, me souffroit acouter
       Joingnant d'elle, près sacouter...
       Et ainsi m'aloit amusant
       Et me souffroit tout raconter,
       Mais ce n'estoit qu'en m'abusant.

67   Abusé m'a et fait entendre
       Tousjours d'un que ce feust ung autre :
       De farine que ce feust cendre,
       D'un mortier un chappel de faultre,
       De viel machefer que feust peaultre,
       D'ambesars que c'estoient ternes
       (Tousjours trompeur autruy engautre
       Et rend vecyes pour lanternes) ;

But do you think this bachelor cove
Would put young bachelorettes aside?
No! Not if he were burned alive
Like one who loves a broomstick ride.*
One whiff of women! Woe betide
The fool who trusts them; he'll admit,   670
Whether they're dark or fair or dyed,
Happy the man who's out of it!

65   If she I served in days gone by
     With such a true and loyal heart,
     The cause of many a tear and sigh
     And so much torment on my part –
     If she had told me at the start
     What she was out for (no hope there!),
     I would have surely learned the art
     Of how to wriggle from the snare.   680

66   Whatever I might want to say,
     She always seemed disposed to hear,
     But not agree or disagree;
     Rather she'd let me snuggle near,
     Where I could whisper in her ear...
     And so she kept me on a string,
     And while I babbled on, my dear
     Bamboozled me in everything.

67   Bamboozled, yes, while in her trap,
     Led to take one thing for another: 690
     Felt bonnet for a judge's cap,
     Any old slag for honest pewter;
     Flour would turn to ash to suit her;
     Threes became aces with her lies
     (It's always that way with a cheater
     Who sells you pincushions for pies);

69

68   Du ciel une paille d'arrain,
    Des nues une peau de veau,
    Du main que c'estoit le serain,
    D'un troingnon de chou ung naviau,
    D'orde servoyse vin nouveau,
    D'une truye ung molin à vent,
    Et d'une hart ung eschevau,
    D'un graz abé ung poursuivant.

69   Ainsi m'ont Amours abusé
    Et pourmené de l'uys au pesle.
    Je croy qu'omme n'est si rusé,
    Fust fin comme argent de coupelle,
    Qui n'y laissast linge, drappelle,
    Mais qu'il fust ainsi manïé
    Comme moy, qui partout m'appelle
    L'amant remis et renÿé.

70   Je regnye Amours et despite
    Et deffie à feu et à sang.
    Mort par elles me precipicte,
    Et ne leur en chault pas d'un blanc.
    Ma vïelle ay mis soubz le banc,
    Amans ne suiveray ja maiz :
    Se jadiz je fuz de leur renc,
    Je declaire que n'en suis maiz.

71   Car j'ay mis le plumail au vent ;
    Or le suive qui a actente !
    De ce me taiz doresnavant,
    Poursuivre je vueil mon entente.
    Et s'aucun me interrogue ou tente
    Comment d'Amours j'ose mesdire,
    Ceste parolle le contente :
    « Qui meurt a ses loix de tout dire. »

68   The sky's a saucepan made of brass,
           The clouds are calfskin, dawn's a sign
           That evening's near and daylight's past;
           Stale beer and cabbage stumps taste fine   700
           Like buttered parsnips and new wine;
           A hangman's rope's a thread of yarn,
           A windmill is a siege machine,
           Fat abbots seem tough men-at-arms.

69   That's how Love tricked me, lured me out,
           Then swiftly locked the door behind;
           I don't think any man's so bright
           (Even like silver twice refined)
           That, fooled like me, he wouldn't find
           That he had lost his shirt and pants,   710
           As I have done, the self-defined
           Renegade Lover who recants.

70   So I renounce all loves, and here
           I challenge them with fire and blood;
           They drive death's chariot hurrying near,
           And don't care who gets splashed with mud.
           I'll pack my fiddle up for good
           And give my lover-friends the slip:
           If in their ranks I ever stood,
           I now resign that fellowship.   720

71   I've cast my feather on the wind,
           May lovers' hopes go where it went;
           On that sore point I've made an end;
           Now I shall say what first I meant.
           If someone calls me to account
           For slandering Love, let me recall
           This proverb: "No one can prevent
           A dying man from telling all".

72   Je congnois approucher ma seuf,
    Je crache blanc comme coton
    Jacoppins groz comme ung estuef.
    Qu'esse à dire ? Que Jehanneton
    Plus ne me tient pour valleton,
    Mais pour ung viel usé rocquart.
    De viel porte voix et le ton,
    Et ne suis q'un jeune cocquart.

73   Dieu mercy — et Tacque Thibault,
    Qui tant d'eaue froide m'a fait boire
    En ung bas, non pas en ung hault,
    Menger d'angoisse mainte poire,
    Enferré. Quant j'en ay memoire,
    Je prie pour luy *et relicqua*
    Que Dieu lui doint, et voire, voire !
    Ce que je pense, *et cetera*.

74   Touteffoiz, je n'y pense mal
    Pour lui et pour son lieutenant,
    Aussi pour son officïal,
    Qui est plaisant et advenant.
    Que faire n'ay du remenant,
    Mais du petit maistre Robert :
    Je les ayme tout d'un tenant,
    Ainsi que fait Dieu le Lombart.

75   Sy me souvient, ad mon advis,
    Que je feiz à mon partement
    Certains laiz, l'an cinquante six,
    Qu'aucuns, sans mon consentement,
    Voulurent nommer 'Testament' ;
    Leur plaisir fut, non pas le myen.
    Mais quoy ! on dit communement :
    « Ung chacun n'est maistre du scien. »

72 I feel a raging thirst that calls;
  With spits of cotton-white, I rain   730
  Down gobs as big as tennis balls.
  What's there to say? That Lady Jane
  Thinks that my powers are on the wane,
  No use for stud, a poor old crock.
  Like some hoarse croaker I complain,
  Yet still I'm only a young cock.

73 Thank God – and Tacque the gay Thibaud,*
  Who made me drink, but not upstairs;
  It was cold water down below,
  In irons, stuffed with his chokepears.* 740
  Now, when I think of it, a prayer
  Springs up for him *et reliqua**
  May God grant him (yes, there! and there!)
  What's in my mind, *et cetera.*

74 And yet I do not bear a grudge
  Against him or his deputy,
  Nor against the presiding judge
  Who's pleasant, always kind to me.
  As for the rest, I let them be,
  Except for little Master Rob: 750
  I love them all quite equally,
  The way the Lombard loves his God.*

75 If I recall, in Fifty-Six,
  I wrote out some bequests, then went
  Away to Angers in the sticks.
  Now some, who don't ask my consent,
  Entitle that a 'Testament' – *
  The choice not mine, but theirs alone.
  Well then! It's what the proverb meant:
  "No man is master of his own".   760

76   Pour les revocquer ne le diz,
         Et y courrust toute ma terre.
         De pictié ne suis reffroydiz
         Envers le Bastard de la Barre :
         Parmi ses troys gluyons de feurre
         Je lui donne mes vielles nattes ;
         Bonnes seront pour tenir serre
         Et soy soustenir sur les pates.

77   S'ainsi estoit qu'aucun n'eust pas
         Receu le laiz que je lui mande,
         J'ordonne qu'après mon trespas
         A mes hoirs en face demande.
         Mais qui sont ilz ? Si le demande
         Morreau, Prouvins, Robin Turgis :
         De moy, dictes que je leur mande,
         Ont eu jusq'au lit où je gis.

78   Somme, plus ne diray q'un mot,
         Car commencer vueil à tester.
         Devant mon clerc Fremin qui m'ot
         (S'il ne dort) je vueil protester
         Que n'entens hommes detester
         En ceste presente ordonnance,
         Et ne la vueil manifester
         Synon ou royaume de France.

79   Je sens mon cueur qui s'affoiblist
         Et plus je ne puis papïer.
         Fremin, siez toy près de mon lit,
         Que l'en ne m'y viengne espïer.
         Pren ancre tost, plume, pappier ;
         Ce que nomme escriptz vistement,
         Puis fay le partout coppïer.
         Et vecy le commancement.

76   Even for all the land I hold,
Not one request would I debar:
My tenderness has not grown cold
Towards the Bastard de la Barre:
Together with three bales of straw,*
I'll give him my old mats thrown in,
So he can bonk upon the floor
And stay more steady on his pins.

77   Now should it happen that someone
Does not receive my old bequest: 770
I bid him, when I'm dead and gone,
To find my heirs with his request.
But who are they? He should address
Robin Turgis, Prouvins, Moreau
And say I told him they possess
Even the bed I lie in now.

78   In short, I'll say just one more thing,
Then start upon my will. Before
My clerk Fremin, who's listening
(If not asleep), I do declare   780
No previous legatee* should fear
Exclusion from this ordinance,
Not to be published anywhere
But in this goodly realm of France.

79   My heart grows weak, my tongue's like lead,
So heavy I can hardly speak.
Fremin, sit close beside my bed,
Lest someone come to spy. Now take
Ink, pen and paper, and be quick
To write what I dictate, and then   790
Send round the copies that you make.
And here begins the *Testament*.

80   Ou nom de Dieu, Pere eternel,
      Et du Filz que Vierge parit,
      Dieu au Pere coeternel
      Ensemble et le Saint Esperit,
      Qui sauva ce qu'Adam perit
      Et du pery parre ses cyeulx —
      Qui bien ce croit peu ne merit :
      Gens mors estre faiz petiz dieux.

81   Mors estoiënt et corps et ames,
      En dampnée perdicïon,
      Corps pourriz et ames en flasmes,
      De quelconque condicïon.
      Touteffoiz fais exepcïon
      Des patriarches et prophetes,
      Car, selon ma concepcïon,
      Oncques grant chaulx n'eurent aux fesses.

82   Qui me diroit : « Qui vous fait mectre
      Si tresavant ceste parolle,
      Qui n'estes en theologie maistre ?
      A vous est presumpcïon folle »,
      C'est de Jhesus la parabolle
      Touchant du Riche ensevely
      En feu, non pas en couche molle,
      Et du Ladre de dessus ly.

83   Se du Ladre eust veu le doyz ardre,
      Ja n'en eust requis reffrigere,
      N'au bout d'icelluy doit aerdre
      Pour raffreschir sa maschoüoire.
      Pÿons y feront macte chierre,
      Qui boyvent pourpoint et chemise.
      Puis que boiture y est si chiere,
      Dieux nous garde de la main mise !

80   In God the Father's name eternal,
      And also, born of Virgin blest,
      The Son, with Father co-eternal,
      Together with the Holy Ghost,
      Who saved all those that Adam lost
      And, raising them to heaven on high,
      (It's good to take all this on trust)
      Made little gods of folk who die.   800

81   Dead were they, soul and body set
      For deep damnation down below,
      Souls flaming as the bodies rot,
      Whatever was their rank. Although
      Prophets and patriarchs,* I know,
      Are not included in the roster,
      Because (I think this must be so)
      Their arses never touched the toaster.

82   If someone asks: "How can this be?
      You preaching this idea to us?   810
      You've no theology degree:
      It's really most presumptuous,"
      It's Jesus' parable I trust,
      About the rich man who was given
      A bed of flames, while Lazarus
      Looked down from his soft couch in Heaven.

83   If he had seen the fingertip
      Of Lazarus burning, he would not
      Have asked for a refreshing sip
      Of water there to cool his throat.   820
      Boozers who'd sell their shirt and coat
      Won't greet the news with loud applause:
      If drink down there's so hard to get,
      God keep us from the Devil's claws!

77

84   Ou nom de Dieu, comme j'ay dit,
        Et de sa glorïeuse Mere,
        Sans pechié soit parfait ce dit
        Par moy, plus maigre que chimere.
        Se je n'ay eu fievre eufumere,
        Ce m'a fait divine clemence,
        Mais d'autre dueil et perte amere
        Je me tais, et ainsi commence.

85   Premier doue de ma povre ame
        La glorïeuse Trinité,
        Et la commande à Nostre Dame,
        Chambre de la Divinité,
        Priant toute la charité
        Des dignes neuf Ordres des cieulx
        Que par eulx soit ce don porté
        Devant le trosne precïeulx.

86   Item, mon corps j'ordonne et laisse
        A nostre grant mere la terre ;
        Les vers n'y trouveront grant gresse :
        Trop lui a fait fain dure guerre.
        Or lui soit delivré grant erre :
        De terre vint, en terre tourne.
        Toute chose, se par trop n'erre,
        Voulontiers en son lieu retourne.

87   Item, et à mon plus que pere,
        Maistre Guillaume de Villon,
        Qui esté m'a plus doulx que mere,
        Enffant eslevé de maillon
        — Degecté m'a de maint boullon,
        Et de cestuy pas ne s'esjoye :
        Sy lui requier à genoullon
        Qu'il m'en laisse toute la joye —

78

84   In God's name, as I said, and in
       That of His own most glorious Mother,
       May I now finish without sin
       This work. I'm thinner now than ever,
       And if I haven't caught the fever,
       It must be heavenly mercy's part.   830
       Of other grief and loss, I'd rather
       Not speak at all; and thus I'll start.

85   First, this poor soul is my bequest
       To the most glorious Trinity,
       Commended to Our Lady blest,
       The Chamber of Divinity,
       Imploring all the charity
       Of heaven's Nine Orders:* they alone
       Should come and bear this gift for me
       Before God's shining precious throne.   840

86   Item, I leave my body to
       Great Mother Earth, where we belong:
       The worms won't find much fat to chew,
       Hunger's assaults were far too strong.
       Give it to her, don't wait too long;
       From earth it came and turns to earth;
       All things, unless I'm very wrong,
       Seek to regain their place of birth.

87   Item, and to my more than father,
       Good Master Guillaume de Villon,   850
       Kinder to this child than a mother,
       My swaddling bands were hardly gone –
       He's often saved me when I ran
       Into some silly scrape. This time
       He's none too pleased; so I kneel down
       And beg him: let the fruit be mine –

88   Je lui donne ma librarye
      Et le *Roumant du Pet au Deable,*
      Lequel maistre Guy Tabarye
      Grossa, qui est homs veritable.
      Par cayeulx est soubz une table ;
      Combien qu'il soit rudement fait,
      La matiere est si tres notable
      Qu'elle admende tout le meffait.

89   Item, donne à ma povre mere,
      Pour saluer nostre Maistresse,
      Qui pour moy ot douleur amere,
      Dieu le scet, et mainte tritresse —
      Autre chastel n'ay ne fortresse
      Où me retraye corps ne ame,
      Quant sur moy court malle destresse,
      Ne ma mere, la povre femme.

Ballade pour prier Nostre Dame

Dame du ciel, regente terïenne,
Emperiere des infernaulx paluz,
Recevez moy, vostre humble crestïenne,
Que comprinse soye entre voz esleuz,
Ce non obstant qu'oncques rien ne valuz.
Les biens de vous, ma Dame, ma Maistresse,
Sont trop plus grans que ne suis pecheresse,
Sans lesquelz biens ame ne peult merir
N'avoir les cieulx : je n'en suis jangleresse :
En ceste foy je vueil vivre et mourir.

A voste Filz dictes que je suis scienne.
De luy soïent mes pechiez aboluz ;
Pardonne moy comme à l'Egipcïenne,
Ou comme il fist au clerc Theophiluz,
Lequel par vous fut quicte et absoluz,

88   To him I give my library
      With *Story of the Devil's Fart*,*
      A tale that Master Tabarie,
      A truthful man, has copied out.   860
      Beneath the table, sheet by sheet,
      It lies; and though the style is crude,
      The subject's worthy of such note
      That it makes up for all that's rude.

89   To my poor mother here I offer
      Something to praise Our Lady's grace;
      God knows the pain she's had to suffer,
      And sorrow caused by my disgrace –
      I have no other fort, no place
      To be my soul and body's haven,   870
      Subjected to this fierce distress;
      Nor has my mother, the poor woman.

Ballade for Praying to Our Lady

Lady of Heaven, Regent of the Earth,
And Empress of the swamps of Hell below,
Receive a humble Christian of no worth
To be among your chosen ones, although
I never counted very much, I know.
The bounties, Sovereign Mistress, of your love
Outweigh the sinfulness of my poor life,
And sure without them (here I tell no lie)   880
There's not a soul that merits heaven above:
And in this faith I mean to live and die.

Tell your dear Son that I am His alone,
Through Him I'll have my sins all washed away,
Like the Egyptian woman, now His own,
Or like the clerk Theophilus* who one day
You ransomed and absolved for good, they say,

81

Combien qu'il eust au deable fait promesse.
Preservez moy que ne face jamaiz ce,
Vierge portant, sans rompture encourir,
Le sacrement c'on celebre à la messe :
En ceste foy je vueil vivre et mourir.

Femme je suis, povrecte et ancïenne,
Qui riens ne sçay : oncques lettres ne leuz.
Au moustier voy, dont suis paroissïenne,
Paradiz paint, où sont harpes et leuz,
Et ung enffer ou dampnez sont bouluz.
L'un me fait paour, l'autre joye et lïesse.
La joye avoir me fait, haulte Deesse,
A qui pecheurs doivent tous recourir,
Comblés de foy, sans faincte ne paresse :
En ceste foy je vueil vivre et mourir.

Vous portastes, digne Vierge, princesse,
Ihesus regnant qui n'a fin ne cesse.
Le Tout Puissant, prenant nostre foiblesse,
Laissa les cieulx et nous vint secourir,
Offrit à mort sa tresclere jeunesse,
Nostre seigneur tel est, tel le confesse :
En ceste foy je veul vivre et mourir.

90   Item, m'amour, ma chiere rose,
Ne luy laisse ne cueur ne foye :
Elle aymeroit mieulx aultre chose,
Combien qu'elle ait assés monnoye.
Quoy ? Une grant bourse de soye,
Plaine d'escuz, parfonde et large ;
Mais pendu soit il que je soye,
Qui luy laira escu ne targe !

Though he had made a promise to the Devil.
Keep me from doing anything so evil,
Virgin intact, within whose womb did lie   890
The sacrament that Mass embodies still:
And in this faith I mean to live and die.

I am a simple woman, poor and old
And ignorant, I never learnt to read.
But in my parish church, there I behold
A painted heaven where harps and lutes are played
And hell where all the damned are boiled and fried.
One brings me fear, the other joy and bliss.
Give me that joy at last, O high Goddess,
On whom we wretched sinners must rely   900
In faith unfeigned and never growing less:
And in this faith I mean to live and die.

Virgin most worthy and our great Princess,
In you lay one whose kingdom cannot cease;
Lord Jesus for our weakness and distress
Left heaven above and, when he chose to die,
Offered his shining youth for our redress.
No other is the Lord that I confess:
And in this faith I mean to live and die.

90   Item, my dearest rose, my love –   910
My heart and liver she won't get:
There's something she'd much rather have,
Although she's far from broke – What's that?
A deep silk purse where she could put
A stash of coin that never fails.
But hang those fools like me who let
That woman have their heads and tails!

91   Car elle en a, sans moy, assés,
       Mais de cela il ne m'en chault :
       Mes plus grans dueilz en sont passés,
       Plus n'en ay le croppïon chault.
       Si m'en desmez aux hoirs Michault
       Qui fut nommé le Bon Fouterre ;
       Priés pour luy, faictes ung sault :
       A Sainct Sathur gist, soubz Sancerre.

92   Ce non obstant, pour m'acquicter
       Envers Amours, plus qu'envers elle,
       — Car oncques n'y peulz acquester
       D'amours une seule estincelle :
       Je ne sçay s'à tous si rebelle
       A esté, ce m'est grant esmoy,
       Mais, par Saincte Marie la Belle,
       Je n'y voy que rire pour moy —

93   Ceste ballade luy envoye
       Qui se termine tout par erre.
       Qui luy portera ? Que je voye…
       Ce sera Pernet de la Barre,
       Pourveu, s'il rencontre en son erre
       Ma damoiselle au nez tortu,
       Il luy dira, sans plus enquerre :
       « Triste paillarde, dont viens tu ? »

Ballade à s'amie

Faulse beaulté qui tant me couste chier,
Rude en effect, ypocrite doulceur,
Amour dure plus que fer à macher,
Nommer que puis, de ma deffaçon seur,
Cherme felon, la mort d'un povre cueur,
Orgueil mussé qui gens met au mourir,
Yeulx sans pitié, ne veult Droit de Rigueur,
Sans empirer, ung povre secourir ?

91 She's fine without me. Well, so what?
  I'm done with all those tears and sighs,
  And now my temperature is not   920
  The only thing that doesn't rise.
  I leave her to old Michault's heirs,
  Alias Shagwell; say a prayer,
  And have a roll down there; he lies
  At Saint-Satur below Sancerre.

92 But still, since I must pay my debt
  To Love, much rather than to her
  – For never could I hope to get
  The slightest spark of passion there;
  Did she put on that modest air   930
  With all men? I am racked by doubt;
  But by St Mary the most fair,
  I don't find much to laugh about –

93 I'll send this absolutely free
  Ballade of lines that end in R,
  Who'll take it to her? Let me see…
  It must be Pernet de la Barre,
  In hope that when he meets my dear,
  My snub-nosed damsel, he will say
  These words into her shell-like ear: 940
  "You slut, whose turn was it today?"

*Ballade to his Ladylove**

False beauty, you whose cost has proved so dear,
Rough in effect, your sweetness fake, I swear,
A love one chews on like an iron bar,
Now I can name it, for my ruin's clear,
Charm that deceives the heart while death is near,
Or lovely eyes that hide a ruthless air;
Indeed, shall not stern justice ever fair
Spare a poor wretch, not drive him to despair?

85

Mieulx m'eust valu avoir esté serchier
Ailleurs secours, c'eust esté mon honneur.
Riens ne m'eust sceu hors de ce fait hacher :
Trocter m'en fault en fuyte et deshonneur.
Haro, haro, le grant et le mineur !
Et qu'esse cy ? Mourray sans coup ferir ?
Ou Pictié veult, selon ceste teneur,
Sans empirer, ung povre secourir ?

Ung temps viendra qui fera dessechier,
Jaunir, flectrir vostre espanye fleur.
Je m'en reisse, se tant peusse macher
Lors ; mais nennil ! Ce seroit donc folleur :
Viel je seray, vous, laide, sans couleur.
Or buvez fort, tant que ru peult courir !
Ne donnez pas à tous ceste douleur :
Sans empirer, ung povre secourir.

Prince amoureux, des amans le greigneur,
Vostre mal gré ne vouldroye encourir,
Mais tout franc cueur doit, par Nostre Seigneur,
Sans empirer, ung povre secourir.

94   Item, à maistre Ythier Marchant,
      Auquel mon branc laissay jadiz,
      Donne (mais qu'il le mecte en chant)
      Ce lay contenant des vers dix,
      (Et au luz) ung *De profundiz*
      Pour ses ancïennes amours,
      Desquelles le nom je ne diz,
      Car il me hairoit à tousjours.

Much better had I listened to my honour   950
And looked for help elsewhere; I have no power
Remaining to break free from this affair:
Take flight I must in shame and in dishonour.
Help, help! I cry to all, both far and near.
Even in death I'll use what arms I bear.
Or shall not Pity, if it lend an ear,
Spare a poor wretch, not drive him to despair?

The day will come when yellow, spoiled and drear
Your full-blown youthful flower must appear.
And then, if I could move my jaws, I'd jeer   960
And laugh. But this is foolish talk, I fear;
I shall be old, you ugly, pale and poor.
So drink your fill, and while it rains I'll pour!
Spread not such pain to all in your career:
Spare a poor wretch, not drive him to despair.

O amorous Prince, truly the greatest lover,
Your high displeasure I would not incur;
But all true hearts that serve Our Lord and Master
Spare a poor wretch, not drive him to despair.

94   Item, to Ythier Marchant,   970
Who had the sword I gave away,*
This lay that's only ten lines long,
Provided that he sees his way
To set it as a lute song, *De
Profundis* for his loves of late,
Whose names I would not dare to say,
On pain of his undying hate.

Lay

Mort, j'appelle de ta rigueur,
Qui m'as ma maistresse ravie
Et n'est pas encore assouvye,
Se tu ne me tiens en langueur.
Oncques puis n'eus force, vigueur.
Mais que te nuysoit elle en vie,
Mort ?

Deux estions et n'avions q'un cueur :
S'il est mort, force est que desvye,
Voirë, ou que vive sans vie,
Comme les ymaiges, par cueur,
Mort.

95   Item, à maistre Jehan Cornu
     Autre nouveau laiz lui vueil faire,
     Car il m'a tousjours subvenu
     A mon grant besoing et affaire.
     Pour ce, le jardin lui transfaire
     Que maistre Pierre Bobignon
     M'arenta, en faisant reffaire
     L'uys et redrecier le pignon.

96   Par faulte d'un huys, g'y perdiz
     Ung grez et ung manche de houe.
     Alors, huit faucons, non pas dix,
     N'y eussent pas prins une aloue :
     L'ostel est seur, mais qu'on le cloue.
     Pour enseigne y mis ung havet,
     Et qui l'ait prins, point ne m'en loue —
     Sanglante nuyt et bas chevet !

88

Lay*

Death, I appeal your stern decree
That stole my mistress from my side,
And nor will you be satisfied   980
Until I languish too and die.
Since then my strength has all gone by;
How did her life your force deride,
Death?

Though we were two, we shared one heart:
Since that is dead, I too must die,
Or lifeless live alone where I
Am but an image, known by heart,
Death.

95   Item, to Master Jean Cornu,   990
I want to make a new bequest,
For he has always pulled me through
When things were at their very worst;
I'll let him have that garden waste
I used to rent from Bobignon,
If he will have the gable raised,
And put the mended door back on.

96   A mattock-shaft and paving stone
Were stolen from me in the dark;
Without that door, I frankly own,   1000
Ten falcons couldn't catch a lark:
And yet the place was safe when locked,
Its sign a meat-hook well in sight –
Whoever took it, may his luck
Be a low bed and bloody night!

97   Item, et pour ce que la femme
Du maistre Piere Saint Amant
(Combien, se coulpe y a à l'ame,
Dieu lui pardonne doulcement !)
Me myt ou ranc de caÿment,
Pour le *Cheval Blanc* qui ne bouge
Lui changay à une jument
Et la *Mulle* à ung asne rouge.

98   Item, donne à Sire Denis
Hyncelin, esleu de Paris,
Quatorze muys de vin d'Aulnys
Prins sur Turgis à mes perilz.
S'il en buvoit tant que periz
En fust son sens et sa raison,
Qu'on mecte de l'eaue es bariz :
Vin pert mainte bonne maison.

99   Item, donne à mon avocat,
Maistre Guillamme Charüau...
Quoy ? Que Marchant ot pour estat :
Mon branc (je me tais du fourreau).
Il aura avec ce ung reau
En change, affin que sa bourse enffle,
Prins sur la chaussée et carreau
De la grant closture du Temple.

100   Item, mon procureur Fournier
Aura pour toutes ses corvées
(Simple sera de l'espargnier)
En ma bourse quatre havées,
Car maintes causes m'a saulvées,
Justes, ainsi Jhesu Crist m'aide !
Comme telles se sont trouvées,
Mais bon droit a bon mestier aide.

97   Item, remembering that the wife
       Of Master Pierre Saint Amant
       (If she has led a sinful life
       May God a tender pardon grant!)
       Once treated me as if I stank,   1010
       I'll swap the old *White Horse* she has
       For some young mare with silken flanks,
       And for her *Mule* give this *Red Ass*.*

98   Item, say fourteen tuns of wine,
       From Turgis and marked down to me,
       I give to Denis Hesselin,
       The exciseman here in Paris.
       And if he drinks so much that he
       Loses his senses, stop and think:
       Water it down; we often see   1020
       A decent house that's wrecked by drink.

99   Item, to Master Charruau,
       My lawyer, what shall I bequeath?
       What Marchant had not long ago,
       My sword erect (forget the sheath!).*
       Also, to bring his purse relief,
       A sovereign's worth of small change, found
       Upon the pavement where the chief
       Templars once had their church and ground.

100   And Fournier, my solicitor,   1030
       Will get four handfuls from my purse
       (He needn't spare it): this is for
       His slog with all those deadly chores,
       Winning for me case after case,
       All of them just, so help me Christ!
       Lawyers who argue a just cause
       Are always the most highly priced.

101   Item, je donne à maistre Jacques
Raguier le *Gran Godet* de Greve,
Pourveu qu'il paiera quatre placques,
Deust il vendre, quoy qu'il lui griefve,
Ce dont on coeuvre mol et greve,
Aler nues jambes, en chappin —
Se sans moy boyt, assiet ne lieve
Au trou de la *Pomme de Pin*.

102   Item, quant est de Merebuef
Et de Nicolas de Louviers,
Vache ne leur donne, ne beuf,
(Car vachiers ne sont ne bouviers),
Mais gans à porter espreviers
(Ne cuidez pas que je me joue !)
Et pour prendre perdrys, ploviers,
Sans faillir sur la Machecoue.

103   Item, viengne Robert Turgis
A moy, je lui paieray son vin ;
Combien, s'il treuve mon logis,
Plus fort fera que le devin.
Le droit lui donne d'eschevin
Que j'ay, comme enffant de Paris.
Se je parle ung poy poictevin,
Ice m'ont deux dames apris.

104   Illes sont très belles et gentes,
Demourant à Saint Generou
Près Saint Julïen de Voventes,
Marche de Bretaigne à Poictou.
Mais i ne di proprement où
Yquelles passent tous les jours.
M'arme ! i ne suy moy si treffou,
Car i vueil celer mes amours.

101   Item, in Place de Grève, *The Goblet*
I give to Jacques Raguier; but first
He'll have to pay four farthings for it,   1040
Even if forced to sell his last
Breeches and go around bare-arsed –
All this, if he dares drink alone,
Standing or sitting, getting pissed
Without me, down in the *Pine Cone*.

102   Item, to Merebuef right now,
And Nicolas de Louviers,
I wouldn't give an ox or cow,
(And they're not cowboys anyway),
But gloves for falconry;* their prey   1050
(It's not a joke, I promise you)
Are quail and plovers on display,
Roasted at Mother Machecoue.

103   Item, if Turgis pays a visit,
I'll pay him for his wine, although
He'll have to find my room (where is it?
Consult some wizard). I bestow
On him the civic rights that go
With a Parisian birth like mine.
And if my speech recalls Poitou,*   1060
Two ladies made it so refined.

104   Real ladies, only fit for gents,
Wiv classy digs at Généroux,
Like near Saint-Julien de Voventes,
Border of Brittany and Poitou;
But still I ain't a-telling you
Just where they doss by night and day;
Cor blimey! Some fings are taboo,
My loves are private anyway.

93

105   Item, à Jehan Raguier je donne
        Qui est sergent, voire des Douze,
        Tant qu'il vivra, ainsi l'ordonne,
        Tous les jours une tallemouze
        Pour boutter et fourrer sa mouse,
        Prinse à la table de Bailly ;
        A Maubué sa gorge arrouse,
        Car au menger n'a pas failly.

106   Item, et au Prince des Sotz
        Pour ung bon sot, Michault du Four,
        Qui à la foyz dit de bons motz
        Et chante bien « Ma doulce amour »,
        Je lui donne, avec le bon jour.
        Brief, mais qu'il fust ung peu en point,
        Il est ung droit sot de sejour
        Et est plaisant où il n'est point.

107   Item, aux Unze Vingt Sergens
        Donne, car leur fait est honneste
        (Et sont bonnes et doulces gens
        Denis Richier et Jehan Valecte)
        A chacun une grant cornecte
        Pour pendre à leurs chappeaux de faultres ;
        J'entends à ceulx à pié, hohecte !
        Car je n'ay que faire des autres.

108   De rechief, donne à Perrenet,
        J'entens le Bastart de la Barre,
        Pource qu'il est beau filz et net,
        En son escu, en lieu de barre,
        Trois dez plombez, de bonne quarre,
        Et ung beau joly jeu de cartes.
        Mais quoy ! s'on l'ot vecir ne poire,
        En oultre aura les fievres quartes.

105   Next, Jean Raguier, if you please,   1070
        A sergeant of the Twelve: now may
        He have for life a daily cheese
        Tart from the table of Bailly.
        I have no doubt that you will see
        His snout get deep into the trough;
        He'll rinse his throat at Maubué,
        For there's no end to what he'll scoff.

106   Item, I give the Prince of Fools
        The very fool he needs to meet,
        Michault du Four, the jokes he tells   1080
        And how he sings 'My love so sweet':
        And now good day, enjoy the treat.
        But in his motley, let's be fair,
        He's the true paragon of wit,
        A charming chap when he's not there.

107   Item, to the Eleven-Score Guard,
        Because they're such an honest set,
        (Gentle and meek, and far from hard,
        Denis Richier and Jean Valette),
        I give a lanyard* that is fit   1090
        To hang... upon their hats – bequest
        Pertaining to the guards on foot:
        I can't care less about the rest.

108   Let's see: the arms of Perrenet,
        (I mean the Bastard de la Barre),
        He's such a fine clean-living guy
        I'll cancel his bar sinister:*
        Instead, three loaded dice will share
        His scutcheon with the ace of hearts.
        What else? Let quartan fever stir   1100
        His guts for every time he farts.

109   Item, ne vueil plus que Chollet
        Dolle, trenche douve ne boise,
        Relie broc ne tonnelet ;
        Mais tous ses houstiz changer voise
        A une espée lionnoise —
        Et retiengne le hutinet :
        Combien qu'il n'ayme bruyt ne noise,
        Sy lui plaist il ung tantinet.

110   Item, je donne à Jehan le Lou,
        Homme de bien et bon marchant,
        Pource qu'il est linget et flou,
        (Et que Cholet est mal serchant)
        Ung beau petit chiennet couchant
        Qui ne laira poullaille en voye.
        Le long tabart est bien cachant
        Pour les mucer, qu'on ne les voye.

111   Item, à l'Orfevre de Boys
        Donne cent clouz, queues et testes,
        De gingembre sarrazinoys,
        Non pas pour accouppler ses boictes,
        Mais pour joindre cuz et couëctes
        Et couldre jambons et andoulles,
        Tant que le let en monte aux tectes
        Et le sang en devalle aux coulles !

112   Au cappitaine Jehan Riou,
        Tant pour lui que pour ses archiers,
        Je donne six hures de lou,
        Qui n'est pas vïande à porchiers,
        Prins à groz matins de bouchiers
        Et cuictes en vin de buffet.
        Pour manger de ces morceaulx chiers,
        On en feroit bien ung mauffait.

109 Item, it's time Cholet* gave up
   Planing and bending wedge and stave
   For keg and firkin, band and hoop;
   But let him swap his adze and shave
   For one good Lyon sword – yet save
   His cooper's mallet: he'll deny
   All love of noise, yet still he'll crave
   A spot of hammering on the sly.

110 Item, to Jean le Loup, good man   1110
   And upright dealer, honest punter,
   Because he's grown so very thin,
   (And Cholet's not much of a hunter),
   I give this dog, a first-class pointer,
   Who'll miss no chickens on the way.
   With that long cloak to hide them under,
   No one will see his latest prey.

111 Item, the Woodsmith* gets from me
   The promise of a hundred spikes –
   Not of the kind that's meant to be   1120
   Used with the fetters that he likes;
   But ginger, giving force that fits
   Sausage to ham and peg to hole,
   So well that milk swells up the tits
   And blood descends into the balls.

112 To Captain Jean Riou I wish,
   For him and for his archers too,
   Six wolfheads, that's a dainty dish
   (Not swineherd's stuff, I promise you:
   But meat that butcher's mastiffs chew),   1130
   Simmered and stewed in sour wine.
   To taste such costly morsels, who
   Would not be tempted into crime?

113   C'est vïande ung peu plus pesante
　　　　Que duvet n'est, plume ne liege.
　　　　Elle est bonne à porter en tante,
　　　　Ou pour user en quelque siege.
　　　　S'ilz estoient prins en ung piege,
　　　　Que ces matins ne seussent courre,
　　　　J'ordonne, moy qui suis son miege,
　　　　Que des peaulx sur l'iver se fourre.

114   Item, à Robinet Trouscaille,
　　　　Qui en service (c'est bien fait)
　　　　A pié ne va comme une caille,
　　　　Mais sur roncin gras et reffait,
　　　　Je lui donne de mon buffet
　　　　Une jacte qu'empruncter n'ose :
　　　　Sy aura mesnage parfait.
　　　　Plus ne lui falloit autre chose.

115   Item, donne à Perrot Girard,
　　　　Barbier juré du Bourg la Royne,
　　　　Deux bacins et ung cocquemart,
　　　　Puis qu'à gaignier mect telle peine.
　　　　Des ans y a demy douzaine
　　　　Qu'en son hostel de cochons gras
　　　　M'apatella une sepmaine,
　　　　Tesmoing l'abesse de Pourras.

116   Item, aux Freres mendïans,
　　　　Aux Devotes et aux Beguines,
　　　　Tant de Paris que d'Orléans,
　　　　Tant Turlupins que Turlupines,
　　　　De graces souppes jacoppines,
　　　　Et flans leur faiz oblacïon,
　　　　Et puis après, soubz ces courtines,
　　　　Parler de contemplacïon.

113   It's somewhat heavier, this meat,
Than feathers, cork or eiderdown;
It's food that soldiers ought to eat
In tents, besieging some poor town.
And if the butcher's wolves were found
In snares, since mastiffs can't be hunters,
Here's my prescription written down: 1140
Let wolfskin serve as fur in winter.

114   For Robin Pressbird (French *Trouscaille*),
Who, on the job (well done, it's said),
Does not go quail-like hopping by
But rides a big fat jade instead:
From my buffet I set aside
A wooden bowl he dare not borrow:
So all his needs are satisfied.
He won't want something else tomorrow.

115   Item, upon Perrot Girard,   1150
Bourg-la-Reine's barber, I bestow
A basin and two bowls that are
Tools of the trade he slaves at so.
I spent a week six years ago
Down at his place being stuffed with fat
Porkers; and at Pourras I know
An abbess* who can swear to that.

116   Item, to all the Mendicant Friars,
To pious women and Béguines,
That Paris or Orleans admires,   1160
Both Turlupins and Turlupines,
Tarts and rich soups called Jacobines
I offer up as an oblation;
And then let the bed curtains screen
Their long discourse of contemplation.

117   Ce ne suis je pas qui leur donne,
        Mais de tous enffans sont les meres,
        Et Dieu, qui ainsi les guerdonne,
        Pour quy seuffrent peines ameres.
        Il fault qu'ilz vivent, les beaulx peres,
        Et mesmement ceulx de Paris :
        S'ilz font plaisirs à noz commeres,
        Ilz ayment ainsi les marys.

118   Quoy que maistre Jehan de Poullieu
        En voulsist dire *et relicqua*,
        Contraint et en publicque lieu,
        Voulsist ou non, s'en revocqua.
        Maistre Jehan de Meun s'en mocqua
        De leur façon ; si fist Mathieu ;
        Mais on doit honnorer ce qu'a
        Honnoré l'Eglise de Dieu.

119   Sy me soubzmectz, leur serviteur
        En tout ce que puis faire et dire,
        A les honnorer de bon cueur
        Et obeïr sans contredire.
        L'omme bien fol est d'en mesdire,
        Car, soit à part ou en prescher
        Ou ailleurs, il ne fault pas dire,
        Ces gens sont pour eulx revanchier.

120   Item, je donne à frere Baude,
        Demourant en l'ostel des Carmes,
        Portant chierre hardie et baude,
        Une sallade et deux guisarmes,
        Que Detusca et ses gens d'armes
        Ne lui riblent sa caige vert :
        Viel est : s'il ne se rent aux armes,
        C'est bien le deable de Vauvert.

117　I'm not the one who grants them this:
　　　Mothers of children, God above,
　　　Choose to reward the friars thus
　　　For everything they strive to give.
　　　All these good fathers have to live　　　　　　1170
　　　(Paris would be their choice); and if
　　　They pleasure wives, it shows their love
　　　To husbands who can't keep it stiff.

118　Whatever Master de Pouilli
　　　Once said of them, the facts remain:
　　　Constrained or not, in public he
　　　Stood up and took it back again.
　　　Matthew and Jean de Meung were seen
　　　To lash their ways with mockery's rod;
　　　Yet one must honour what has been　　　　　　1180
　　　So honoured by the Church of God.

119　So I submit and, for my part,
　　　In everything I do and say
　　　I'll honour them with all my heart,
　　　Not contradict them but obey.
　　　Only a madman, anyway,
　　　Would bitch about them; you should not,
　　　Aloud or whispering, ever say:
　　　"Friars are a vindictive lot."

120　Item, I give to Friar Baude,　　　　　　1190
　　　Still dwelling with the Carmelites,
　　　Known by his bearing brave and bold,
　　　A helmet and two halberds bright;
　　　So that Detusca's men take fright,
　　　And leave the *Green Cage** in his care:
　　　He's old; if he still wants to fight,
　　　He's the real devil of Vauvert.*

121   Item, pour ce que le Seelleur
        Maint estront de mouche a machié,
        Donne, car homme est de valleur,
        Son seau d'avantaige crachié,
        Et qu'il ait le poulce escachié
        Pour tout empreindre à une voye ;
        J'entens celluy de l'Eveschié,
        Car les autres, Dieu les pourvoye !

122   Quant des auditeurs messeigneurs,
        Leur granche ilz auront lambroissée,
        Et ceulx qui ont les culz rongneux,
        Chacun une chaize persée ;
        Mais qu'à la petite Macee
        D'Orléans, qui ot ma seinture,
        L'amende en soit bien hault tauxée :
        Elle est une mauvaise ordure.

123   Item, donne à maistre Françoys,
        Promocteur, de la Vacquerie,
        Ung hault gorgerin d'Escossoys,
        Touteffoys sans orfaverie,
        Car, quant receut chevallerye,
        Il maugrea Dieu et saint George
        (Parler n'en oit qui ne s'en rie)
        Comme enraigé, à plaine gorge.

124   Item, à maistre Jehan Laurens,
        Qui a les povres yeulx si rouges
        Pour le pechié de ses parens
        Qui boivent en baris et courges,
        Je donne l'envers de mes bouges
        Pour tous les matins les torcher.
        S'il fust arcevesque de Bourges,
        Du cendail eust, mais il est cher.

121 Item, to one who keeps the Seal,
     Condemned to eat what bees must shit
     (Since he's a decent man, I feel),   1200
     I give a seal made wet with spit;
     And may his thumb be squashed quite flat
     To make the stamp with just one punch –
     I mean the bishop's seal, that's it:
     I leave to God the other bunch!

122 My lords the auditors will get
     Some wooden panels for their den;
     And those with mangy bums will sit
     On pretty privy seats, each one.
     But first Macée of Orléans   1210
     Who stole my money belt – he, she, or it
     Should have to pay some whacking fine,
     The nasty little piece of shit!

123 I give the prosecutor knight,
     Sir François de la Vacquerie,
     A Scottish gorget, one that's quite
     Plain and has no gold filigree;
     For when he entered chivalry,
     He cursed St George and even God:
     One can't but laugh to hear how he   1220
     Was dubbed and drubbed, and screamed like mad.

124 To Jean Laurens, whose eyes are red
     Because his parents were so sinful
     They'd drink from barrel or from gourd,
     Or anything to get a skinful,
     I give this sackcloth as a windfall –
     The rough side's best to wipe them dry.
     Were he archbishop, I am mindful,
     The cost of silk might be too high.

125   Item, à maistre Jehan Cotart,
Mon procureur en court d'Eglise,
Devoye environ ung patart
(Car à present bien m'en advise),
Quant chicaner me feist Denise,
Disant que l'avoye mauldicte.
Pour son ame, qu'es cieulx soit mise,
Ceste orroison j'ay cy escripte :

Ballade pour Jehan Cotart

Pere Noé, qui plantastes la vingne,
Vous aussi, Loth, qui bustes ou rocher
Par tel party qu'Amours, qui gens engingne,
De voz filles si vous fist approucher
(Pas ne le dy pour le vous reproucher),
Archedeclin, qui bien seustes cest art —
Tous troys vous pry que vous vueillez prescher
L'ame du bon feu maistre Jehan Cotart.

Jadis extraict il fut de vostre ligne,
Lui qui buvoit du meilleur et plus cher,
Et ne deust il avoir vaillant ung pigne :
Certes, sur tous, c'estoit ung bon archer :
On ne lui sceut pot des mains arracher :
De bien boire ne feut oncques fetart.
Nobles seigneurs, ne souffrez empescher
L'ame du bon feu maistre Jehan Cotart !

Comme homme viel qui chancelle et trespigne
L'ay veu souvent, quant il s'alloit coucher,
Et une foiz il se fist une bigne,
Bien m'en souvient, pour la pie juchier.
Brief, on n'eust sceu en ce monde sercher
Meilleur pïon, pour boire tost et tart.
Faites entrer, quant vous orrez hucher,
L'ame du bon feu maistre Jehan Cotart !

125   To Jean Cotart, my council in   1230
          The high ecclesiastical court,
          I owe two farthings that have been
          Due since the action that he fought
          Against Denise, who said I'd sought
          To lay a curse on her, she'd swear.
          In hope that his good soul be brought
          To heaven, I composed this prayer:

Ballade for Jean Cotart

Noah, good father, planter of the vine,
And Lot as well who drank inside the cave
So deep that Love who tricks the best of minds   1240
Urged you towards your daughters to make love
(Not something that I'll make an issue of),
Architriclinus, Cana's connoisseur –
All three, I beg you, welcome up above
The soul of our good Master Jean Cotart.

For this distinguished issue of your line
Only the best was ever good enough,
And even when he hadn't got a bean
He'd still be downing the most pricey stuff;
No boozer ever could outdrink the chief,   1250
You couldn't tear his fingers from the jar.
Let nothing, lords, prevent you, but reprieve
The soul of our good Master Jean Cotart!

After some late-night binge I've often seen
Him stumbling, staggering home to sleep it off;
Once, I recall, the bedpost was so mean
It gave his addled head a frightful biff.
For drinking late or early, who could have
A better mate? – there's no one near or far.
When the call comes, throw open to receive   1260
The soul of our good Master Jean Cotart!

Prince, il n'eust sceu jusqu'à terre cracher.
Tousjours crioit. « Haro ! La gorge m'art ! »
Et ne sceut onc sa seuf estancher
L'ame du bon feu maistre Jehan Cotart.

126   Item, vueil que le jeune Marle
Desormaiz gouverne mon change,
Car de changer enviz me mesle,
Pourveu que tousjours baille en change,
Soit à privé ou à estrange,
Pour troys escus six brectes targes,
Pour deux angelotz ung grant ange,
Car amans doivent estre larges.

127   Item, et j'ay sceu, ce voyaige,
Que mes troys povres orphelins
Sont creuz et deviennent en aage
Et n'ont pas testes de belins,
Et qu'enffans d'icy à Salins
N'a mieulx saichant leur tour d'escolle.
Or, par l'ordre des Mathelins,
Telle jeunesse n'est pas folle.

128   Sy vueil qu'ilz voisent à l'estude —
Où ? Sur maistre Pierre Richier.
Le *Donat* est pour eulx trop rude :
Ja ne les y vueil empescher.
Ilz sauront (je l'ayme plus cher)
Ave salus, tibi decus,
Sans plus grans lettres enserchier :
Tousjours n'ont pas clercs l'au dessus.

He'd cry "My throat's on fire!" and didn't have
The spit enough, my Prince, to hit the floor.
Nothing could quench that thirst, that craving of
The soul of our late Master Jean Cotart.

126   Item, I want young Marle to be
My business-manager from now on,
Exchange is not the job for me:
But then the rate that he lays down
Should be the same for everyone: 1270
One guinea buys six bob, as listed,
And fifty pence gets half-a-crown,*
For lovers shouldn't be tight-fisted.

127   Item, I learnt while on this trip
My three poor orphans* are no clowns;
No boneheads they, but growing up
Surely the smartest kids around:
From here to Salins can't be found
Young salts who've learnt so much at school.
Now, by St Mathurin, renowned   1280
For curing folly, they're no fools.

128   Those studies, where to round them off?
With Master Richier, that's where.
Donatus would be far too tough
And would confuse their minds, I fear.
What they should learn (I hold it dear)
Is *Ave salus, tibi decus*.* Drop
All books right there: it's far from clear
That scholars will come out on top.

129   Cecy estudient, et ho !
           Plus proceder je leur deffens.
           Quant d'entendre le grant *Credo*,
           Trop forte elle est pour telz enffans.
           Mon grant tabart en long je fens :
           Sy vueil que la moictié s'en vende
           Pour eulx en achecter des flans,
           Car jeunesse est ung peu friande.

130   Sy vueil qu'ilz soient informez
           En meurs, quoy que couste basture.
           Chapperons aront enformez
           Et les poulces sur la sainture,
           Humbles à toute creature,
           Disans : « Han ? Quoy ? Il n'en est rien ! »
           Sy diront gens par adventure :
           « Vecy enffans de lieu de bien ! »

131   Item, à mes povres clergons,
           Ausquelz mes tiltres resigné,
           Beaux enffans et droiz comme joncs —
           Les voyant m'en dessaisiné,
           Sans recevoir leur assigné,
           Seur comme qui l'aroit en paulme,
           A ung certain jour consigné,
           Sur l'ostel de Gueuldry Guillaume.

132   Quoy que jeunes et esbatans
           Soient, en riens ne m'en desplaist ;
           Dedens trente ans ou quarante ans
           Bien autres seront, se Dieu plaist.
           Il fait mal qui ne leur complest,
           Ilz sont tresbeaulx enffans et gens ;
           Et qui les bat ne fiert fol est,
           Car enffans si deviennent gens.

129   So let them study that, then Whoa!   1290
       All further learning I forbid.
       Credo or credit is, I know,
       Too difficult for these poor kids.
       My great long cloak I shall divide
       In two, and sell the larger part
       To buy some pastries on the side:
       Young people have a taste for tarts.

130   Good manners also they should learn,
       Though it may cost a clout or two:
       They'll go around with hoods pulled down   1300
       And thumbs in belts as hoodies do,
       Humble to all, both high and low,
       With "Well?", "Whatever", "No, not quite."
       So folk perhaps will say: "There go
       Youngsters whose family got it right."

131   Item, the lads to whom I cede
       My titles, my poor under-clerks,*
       Handsome young fellows, straight as reeds –
       The sight of them! I took one look,
       And thought: right now this gift I'll make: 1310
       As if it were in hand already,
       The land rent will be theirs to take
       On the house of Guillaume Gueutry.

132   Young lads may sometimes make a row,
       It doesn't worry me at all;
       Some thirty, forty years from now
       They'll be quite different, with God's will.
       It's sinful not to treat them well:
       They're fine upstanding chaps; and then
       To beat them is to be a fool,   1320
       For soon these kids will be grown men.

133   Les bources des Dix et Huit Clercs
    Aront ; je m'y vueil traveillier.
    Pas ilz ne dorment comme loirs,
    Qui troys moys sont sans resveillier.
    Auffort, triste est le sommeillier
    Qui fait aise jeune en jeunesse,
    Tant qu'en fin lui faille veillier
    Quant reposer deust en viellesse.

134   Sy en rescriptz au collateur
    Lettres semblables et parreilles ;
    Or prient pour leur bien faicteur,
    Ou qu'on leur tire les orreilles.
    Aucunes gens ont grans merveilles
    Que tant m'encline vers ces deulx,
    Mais, foy que doy festes et veilles,
    Oncques ne vy les meres d'eulx !

135   Item, donne à Michault Cul d'Oue
    Et à sire Charlot Tarrenne
    Cent solz (s'ilz demandent : « Prins où ? »
    Ne leur chaille : ilz vendront de manne)
    Et une houlse de basenne,
    Autant empeigne que semelle,
    Pourveu qu'ilz me salueront Jehanne,
    Et autant une autre comme elle.

136   Item, au Seigneur de Grigny,
    Auquel jadiz lessay Vissextre,
    Je donne la tour de Billy,
    Pourveu, s'huys y a ne fenestre
    Qui soit ne debout ne en estre,
    Qu'il mecte tresbien tout à point.
    Face argent à destre et senestre,
    Il m'en fault et il n'en a point.

133   They'll have the stipends granted to
       The Eighteen Clerks, I'll work it out.
       For they don't sleep as dormice do,
       Three months a year – of course, they're right:
       It's sad to see how sweet and tight
       A young man sleeps until, at last,
       He has to stay awake all night
       When he is old and needs a rest.

134   I wrote the same recommendation   1330
       For both, verbatim, to be fair;
       Now they should pray for my salvation,
       Or else someone should pull their ears.
       Some people wonder why this pair
       Are dear to me above all others;
       But by all feasts and fasts I swear
       I never even knew their mothers!

135   Item, I give Michel Culdoe
       And likewise Sir Charlot Tarrenne a
       Hundred *sous* (don't ask me how   1340
       I get them; they'll just fall like manna);
       And leather boots, well worth a tanner,
       The soles and uppers rather frayed –
       But they must greet in my old manner
       Big Joan and one who shares her trade.

136   To Grigny's lord some years ago
       I left Bicêtre;* now I might
       Add Billy tower, but I must know
       That where a window sheds no light
       Or door no longer stands upright,   1350
       He'll fix it up before he's done.
       Let him make money left and right;
       I need some badly, he's got none.

137   Item, à Thibault de la Garde…
Thibault ? Je mens : il a nom Jehan !
Que lui donrai ge que ne perde ?
(Assez j'ay perdu tout cest an ;
Dieu y vueille pourvoir, amen !)
Le *Barillet* ? Par m'ame, voire !
Genevoys est plus ancïen
Et plus beau nez a pour y boire.

138   Item, je donne à Basennier
Noctaire et greffier criminel,
De giroffle plain ung panier
Prins sur maistre Jehan de Rüeil,
Tant à Mautaint, tant à Rosnel,
Et, avec ce don de girofle,
Servir de cueur gent et ysnel
Le seigneur qui sert saint Christofle,

139   Auquel ceste ballade donne
Pour sa dame, qui tous biens a.
S'Amour ainsi tous ne guerdonne,
Je ne m'esbahys de cela,
Car au pas conquester l'ala
Que tint Regnier, roy de Cecille,
Où si bien fist et peu parla
C'oncques Hector fist ne Troille.

Ballade pour Robert d'Estouteville

Au point du jour, que esprevier s'esbat,
Meu de plaisir et par noble coustume,
Bruyt la mauviz et de joyë s'esbat,
Reçoyt son per et se joinct à sa plume,
Offrir vous vueil, ad ce desir m'alume,
Joyeusement ce qu'aux amans bon semble :
Sachiez qu'Amour l'escript en sa volume,
Et c'est la fin pourquoy sommes ensemble.

137 Now Thibaud de la Garde gets this...
     Thibaud? I'm lying. He's called John!
     What can I give that I won't miss?
     (I've lost too much this year that's gone:
     May God provide for me, Amen).
     The Keg? On second thoughts, I'd choose
     Genevois, he's the older man   1360
     And has the better nose for booze.

138 Item, to Basennier, notary
     And registrar of crimes, this nice
     Full bag of cloves in hope that he
     Will perk up with a touch of spice,
     And Mautant and Roisnel likewise;
     And with these cloves I also offer
     Your loyal service to that wise
     Lord who still serves St Christopher,

139 To whom I give this ballade for   1370
     His lady, heir to all the graces;
     If Love rewards him so much more
     Than other men, the more his praise is.
     In jousting for this best of prizes
     Before fair Sicily's King René
     He spoke few words, but fought in ways as
     Bold as were Hector's in his day.

*Ballade for Robert d'Estouteville**

As day breaks and the falcon claps his wings,
Moved by good custom to his joyous flight,
Blithely the throstle takes the air and sings,   1380
Ruffling her feathers to receive her mate;
Oh then, urged on by passion and delight,
I long to offer you what pleases lovers:
Such is the law that Love sets down as right,
Ever the end for which we are together.

Dame serez de mon cueur sans debat,
Entierement, jusques mort me consume,
Lorrier soüef qui pour mon droit combat,
Olivier franc m'otant toute amertume.
Raison ne veult que je desacoustume
(Et en ce vueil avec elle m'assemble)
De vous servir, mais que m'y acoustume,
Et c'est la fin pourquoy sommes ensemble.

Et qui plus est, quant dueil sur moy s'embat
Par Fortune, qui souvent si se fume,
Vostre doulx œil sa malice rabat,
Ne plus ne moins que le vent fait la fume.
Sy ne pers pas la graine que je sume
En vostre champ, quant le fruyt me ressemble.
Dieu m'ordonne que le fouÿsse et fume,
Et c'est la fin pourquoy sommes ensemble.

Princesse, oëz ce que cy vous resume :
Que le mien cueur de vostre desassemble
Ja ne sera ; tant de vous en presume,
Et c'est la fin pourquoy sommes ensemble.

140 Item, à sire Jehan Perdrier,
Riens, n'à Françoys son second frere ;
Sy m'ont voulu tousjours aidier
Et de leurs biens faire confrere —
Combien que Françoys, mon compere,
Langue cuisans, flambans et rouges,
My commandement my priere,
Me recommanda fort à Bourges.

Deep will you be, dear lady, in my heart
Entire, unquestioned, till my dying day,
Laurel who sweetly combats for my right,
Olive that takes all bitterness away;
Right reason tells me that I should not stray   1390
(Easily I consent to this endeavour),
But keep on serving you in every way,
And that's the end for which we are together.

And what is more, when sorrow casts me down
And Fortune's malice holds me in its spell,
Your sweet calm eye deflects that angry frown,
Mere smoke and vapour that the wind dispels.
The seed sown in your field's not lost: it swells
Into a fruit, my image in another.
God tells me: dig and fertilize it well,   1400
And that's the end for which we are together.

Listen, Princess, while I repeat this theme:
It cannot be that anything should sever
My heart from yours; I think your heart's the same:
And that's the end for which we are together.

140   Item, to Sir Jean Perdrier – nowt;
Nor to his younger brother Francis.
Although they've always helped me out
And shared their goods and lucky chances –
But my pal Frank has some strange fancies: 1410
Eating at Bourges, "Try this," he said,
(Almost an order), then advances
Fried tongues, hot-spiced and flaming red.

141   Sy alé voir en Taillevant,
Ou chappitre de fricassure,
Tout au long, derriere et devant,
Lequel n'en parle jus ne sure.
Mais Macquaire, je vous asseure,
A tout le poil cuisant ung deable
Afin qu'il sentist bon l'arseure,
Ce *recipe* m'escript sans fable.

Ballade des langues ennuieuses

En rïagal, en alcenic rocher,
En orpiment, en salpestre et chaulx vive,
En plomb boulant pour mieulx les esmorcher,
En suye et poix destrempée de lessive
Faictes d'estront et de pissat de Juisve,
En lavailles de jambes à meseaux,
En raclure de piez et vieulx houzeaux,
En sang d'aspic et drocques venimeuses,
En fiel de loups, de regnars, de blereaux,
Soient frictes ces langues ennuyeuses !

En servelle de chat qui hait pescher,
Noir, et si viel qu'il n'ait dent en gencyve ;
D'un viel matin, qui vault bien aussi chier,
Tout enraigé en sa bave et sallive,
En l'escume d'une mulle poussive,
Detrenchée menue à bons cyseaux,
En eaue où ratz plungent groins et museaux,
Regnes, crappaulx et bestes dangereuses,
Serpens, laissars et telz nobles oiseaux,
Soient frictes ces langues ennuyeuses !

En sublimé, dangereux à toucher,
Et ou nombril d'une couleuvre vive,
En sang c'on voit es poillectes sechier

141 Would Taillevant have what I want?
   I looked up "Fry" and read it through,
   From end to end and back to front,
   And still found nothing that would do;
   And yet Macquaire, who'd like to stew
   A hairy devil in his pot
   Just for the smell, wrote down this true   1420
   Old recipe, I kid you not:

    Ballade of Malicious Tongues*

   In sulphurous arsenic and powdered stone
   In orpiment, saltpetre and quicklime,
   In boiling lead, better to melt them down,
   In pitch and soot, with lye, and in a slime
   Of Jewish piss and shit at the same time,
   In water from the bath where lepers meet,
   In scrapings from the soles of shoes or feet,
   In viper's blood, each venom earth provides,
   In gall that badger, fox and wolf secrete,   1430
   – In this let such malicious tongues be fried!

   In brains of some black cat that hates to fish,
   So old he has no tooth left in his gums;
   Or, if some rabid mastiff grace the dish,
   In slobber and the filthy drool that comes
   Out of his jaws, or in the frothy scum
   Skimmed from a mule hacked into tiny bits;
   In water long the home of muzzling rats,
   Where frogs and toads resort from far and wide,
   Lizards and serpents, noble beasts like that,   1440
   – In this let such malicious tongues be fried!

   In sublimates too dangerous to touch,
   In navel of a snake that's still alive,
   With blood the full moon dries in basins which

Sur ces barbiers, quant plaine lune arrive,
Dont l'un est noir, l'autre plus vert que cyve,
En chancre et fix et en ces ors cuveaulx
Où nourrisses essangent leurs drappeaux,
En petits baings de filles amoureuses
(Qui ne m'entant n'a suivy les bordeaux)
Soient frictes ces langues ennuyeuses !

Prince, passez tous ces frians morceaux
S'estamine, sacs n'avez ne bluteaux,
Parmy le fons d'unes brayes breneuses ;
Mais paravant en estronc de pourceaux
Soient frictes ces langues ennuyeuses !

142   Item, à maistre Andry Courault
       Les *Contreditz Franc Gontier* mande ;
       Quant du tirant seant en hault,
       A cestuy là riens ne demande :
       Le Saige ne veult que contende
       Contre puissant povre homme las,
       Affin que ses filletz ne tende
       Et qu'il ne trebuche en ses las.

143   Gontier ne crains : il n'a nulz hommes,
       Et mieulx que moy n'est herité ;
       Mais en ce debat cy nous sommes
       Car il loue sa pouvreté,
       Estre povre yver et esté,
       Et à felicité reppute
       Ce que tiens à maleureté.
       Lequel a tort ? Or en discute.

Barbers display because they hope to thrive
(Some blood turns black, some greener than a chive);
In pestilent pustules and venereal sores,
In tubs where nappies soak, tin baths where scores
Of girls wash out what love has left inside
(If you don't get me, you're no friend of whores)   1450
– In this let such malicious tongues be fried!

Prince, take this tasty mixture, strain it through
A sack or filter, but if that won't do,
A pair of drawers, somewhat brown inside;
But first a dash of pig shit in the brew
– In this let such malicious tongues be fried!

142   Item, for Master Courault I
      Send my retort to Gontier.*
      As for the tyrant throned on high,
      To him there's nothing I can say: 1460
      The Sage has said the poor man's way
      Is not to argue with the great,
      Lest he should stumble just where they
      Have placed the snares that lie in wait.

143   I don't fear Gontier, he has
      No men and no more wealth than me,
      But this debate has come on us
      Because he praises poverty;
      In winter and in summer he
      Considers perfect happiness   1470
      What I regard as misery.
      Now which of us is wrong? Discuss.

Ballade, *Les Contredits Franc Gontier*

Sur mol duvet assiz, ung gras chanoine,
Lez ung brasier, en chambre bien natée,
A son costé gisant dame Sidoine,
Blanche, tendre, polye et attintée,
Boire ypocras à jour et à nuytée,
Rire, jouer, mignonner et baisier,
Et nud à nud, pour mieulx des corps s'aisier —
Les vy tous deux par ung trou de mortaise.
Lors je congneuz que, pour dueil appaisier,
Il n'est tresor que de vivre à son aise.

Se Franc Gontier et sa compaigne Elayne
Eussent ceste doulce vie hantée,
D'oignons, cyvotz, qui causent forte alaine,
N'acontassent une bise tostée.
Tout leur maton, ne toute leur potée
Ne prise ung ail, je le dy sans noisier.
Sy se vantent couchier soubz le rosier !
Lequel vault mieulx ? Lit costoyé de cheze ?
Qu'en dictes vous ? Fault il ad ce muser ?
Il n'est tresor que de vivre à son aise.

De groz pain bis vivent, d'orge e d'avoyne,
Et boyvent eaue tout au long de l'année.
Tous les oyseaux de cy en Babiloyne
A tel escolle une seulle journée
Ne me tendroient, non une matinée.
Or s'esbate, de par Dieu, Franc Gontier,
Helayne o luy, soubz le bel esglantier :
Si bien leur est, cause n'ay qu'il me poise ;
Mais, quoy que soit du laboureux mestier,
Il n'est tresor que de vivre à son aise.

Ballade Refuting Franc Gontier

A sleek fat canon on an eiderdown,
Thick carpets wall to wall, a jolly fire,
And lolling by his side good Dame Sidoine,
Smooth, tender, white, dolled up for his desire,
With wine well spiced to lift their spirits higher,
Laughing and kissing, tickling just in play,
Stark naked both of them, more fun that way –
Watching them through a chink, one truth I seize,   1480
That when it comes to chasing cares away
Nothing compares with living at your ease.

If Gontier with Elaine for his companion
Could ever put that sweet life to the test,
They wouldn't spoil their breath with chive and onion,
Stuff that's not worth a frazzled slice of toast.
Their pot of curds and whey and all the rest
Rates less than garlic. As for sleeping out
Under the rose trees that they boast about,
Think of a comfy bed and armchair, please.   1490
What do you reckon? Must I spell it out?
Nothing compares with living at your ease.

Water's their only drink throughout the year,
Oats, barley and brown bread make up their diet.
Not all the birds from Babylon to here
Would ever be enough to make me buy it,
Not for one day, one morning, would I try it.
So let Franc Gontier take his fill of pleasure
Under the hawthorn with Elaine his treasure;
No problem, let them frolic as they please.   1500
Still, for all that laborious rustic leisure,
Nothing compares with living at your ease.

Prince, jugiez, pour tost nous accorder.
Quant est de moy, mais qu'à nulz ne desplaise,
Petit enffant, j'ay oÿ recorder :
Il n'est tresor que de vivre à son aise.

144   Item, pour ce que scet sa Bible
       Madamoiselle de Bruyeres,
       Donne prescher hors l'Euvangille
       A elle et à ses bachelieres,
       Pour retraire ces villotieres
       Qui ont bec si affilé,
       Mais que ce soit hors cymetieres,
       Trop bien au Merchié au fillé.

Ballade des femmes de Paris

Quoy qu'on tient belles langaigieres
Florentines, Venicïennes,
Assés pour estre messaigieres,
Et mesmement les ancïennes,
Mais soiënt Lombardes, Roumaines,
Genevoyses, à mes perilz,
Pimontoises, Savoysïennes,
Il n'est bon bec que de Paris.

De beau parler tiennent chayeres,
Ce dit on, les Neappolitaines,
Et que bonnes sont cacquetieres
Allemandes et Prucïennes.
Soient Grecques, Egipcïennes,
De Hongrie ou d'autre pays,
Espaignolles ou Castellanes,
Il n'est bon bec que de Paris.

Prince, you decide between us, we'll obey.
I only state (I hope it won't displease)
That as a lad I often heard men say:
Nothing compares with living at your ease.

144   Item, because she knows her Bible,
I give to Mistress de Bruyères,
The right to take her girl-disciples
And teach the Gospel everywhere;   1510
And more precisely to those fair
Streetwalkers who are sharp of tongue –
And not in graveyards, but out there
In markets where such trades belong.

Ballade of the Women of Paris

They say that Florence is the scene
For ladies who enjoy a natter;
Venice is good for go-betweens
(Even the oldies know the patter);
Romans and Lombards love to chatter,
Genoese girls have repartee;   1520
Piedmont, Savoy – it doesn't matter:
For gab there's only Gay Paree.

In Naples women hold the chairs
Of eloquence and rhetoric,
Prussian and German Fräuleins share
A way of speech that's very slick;
Greeks and Egyptians know the trick,
They've learnt it too in Hungary;
But though I grant they're pretty quick,
For gab there's only Gay Paree.   1530

Brectes, Souyssez ne scevent guerres,
Gasconnes ne Toulousïennes :
De Petit Pont deux harengieres
Les concluront, et les Lorraines,
Angleches et Callesïennes
(Ai ge beaucoup de lieux compris ?)
Picardes de Vallencïennes.
Il n'est bon bec que de Paris.

Prince, aux dames Parisïennes
De beau parler donnez le pris ;
Quoy qu'on die d'Italïennes,
Il n'est bon bec que de Paris.

145   Regarde m'en deux, troys, assises
Sur le bas du ply de leurs robes,
En ces moustiers, en ces eglises ;
Tire t'en près, et ne te hobes :
Tu trouveras là que Macrobes
Oncques ne fist telz jugemens.
Entens, quelque chose en desrobes :
Ce sont tous beaux enseignemens.

146   Item, et au mont de Montmartre,
Qui est ung lieu moult ancïen,
Je lui donne et adjoincts le tertre
Qu'on dit de Mont Valerÿen ;
En oultre plus, ung quartier d'an
Du pardon qu'apportay de Romme.
Sy yra maint bon chrestïen
En l'abbaye où il n'entre homme.

Irish colleens* may boast their blarney –
Two fishwives on the Petit-Pont
Would slang them speechless in a barney;
Bretons aren't glib, and Swiss are glum,
And English girls are rather dumb,
Don't try Lorraine or Picardy,
(Tell me, have I forgotten some?)
For gab there's only Gay Paree.

Prince, give the prize for eloquence
To our Parisian dames; you'll see   1540
Italians never stand a chance:
For gab there's only Gay Paree.

145   See them in groups of two or three,
Squatting in skirts that sweep the ground
In chapel, church, or sanctuary;
Draw near, don't budge or make a sound.
Macrobius was not renowned
For judgements such as these. Just listen.
You'll pick up something, I'll be bound:
Nothing but very proper lessons.   1550

146   Item, Montmartre and its nuns,
Ancient enough by all accounts:
They get the hill Valerïen
That (God knows why) men call a mount.
What's more, I place on their account
Three months' indulgence* fresh from Rome,
So Christian men, with that amount,
May go where men have never come.

147 Item, varletz et chamberieres
De bon hostelz (rien ne me nuyt !)
Faisans tartes, flans et goyeres
Et grans ralïatz à myenuyt
(Rien n'y font sept pints ne huit
Tant que gisent seigneur et dame) ;
Puis après, sans mener grant bruyt,
Je leur ramentoy le jeu d'asne.

148 Item, et à filles de bien,
Qui ont peres, meres et antes,
Par m'ame, je ne donne rien,
Car j'ay tout donné aux servantes.
Sy feussent ilz de peu contentes :
Grant bien leur feissent mains loppins
Aux povres filles entrementes
Qu'ilz se perdent aux Jacoppins,

149 Aux Celestins et aux Chartreux ;
Quoy que vie mainent estroicte,
Sy ont ilz largement entre eulx
Dont povres filles ont souffrecte,
Tesmoing Jacquelin et Perrecte,
Et Ysabeau qui dit : « Enné ! »
Puisqu'ilz en ont telle disecte,
A peine seroit on dampné.

150 Item, à la Grosse Margot,
Tres doulce face et pourtraicture,
— Foy que doy, *brulare bigot*,
A si devocte creature —
Je l'ayme de propre nature
Et elle moy, la doulce sade.
Qui la trouvera d'aventure,
Qu'on lui lise ceste ballade.

147   Item, let men and maids who serve
       (In the best households, I should state),   1560
       Make midnight feasts where rich preserves
       And tarts and pies load every plate,
       Washed down by seven pints or eight,
       While lord and lady slumber sound:
       Then my advice is: have a late
       Ballgame, but keep the noises down.

148   Item, to maidens prim and proper,
       With fathers, mothers, aunts as well,
       There's nothing left that I can offer,
       The servant-girls have had it all.   1570
       Yet there's a morsel not too small
       Would do those maids a power of good,
       Each one would get a bellyful,
       If friars did just what they should;

149   Or else take Celestine, Carthusian:
       However strict the life they lead,
       They still possess in great profusion
       Just what those poor girls really need;
       Ask Isabelle who says: "Indeed!"
       With Jacqueline and young Perrette: 1580
       Their garden is so starved of seed
       They won't be damned for what they get.

150   Item, my sweet-faced Fat Margot,
       Just like a picture on display, –
       So help me! By the faith I owe,
       Devoted creature, I must say –
       I love her well in my own way
       And, softie, she loves me, no doubt.
       If you should come across her, stay
       With her and read this ballad out.   1590

Ballade de la Grosse Margot

Se j'ayme et sers la belle de bon het,
M'en devez vous tenir ne vil ne sot ?
Elle a en soy des biens à fin soubzhet ;
Pour son amour seins boucler et passot.
Quant viennent gens, je cours et happe ung pot,
Au vin m'en voys, sans demener grant bruyt ;
Je leur tens eaue, froumaige, pain et fruyt.
S'ilz paient bien, je leur diz « *bene stat* ;
Retournez cy, quant vous serez en ruyt,
En ce bordeau où tenons nostre estat. »

Mais adoncques il y a grant deshet,
Quant sans argent s'en vient coucher Margot :
Voir ne la puis, mon cueur à mort la het.
Sa robe prens, demy seint et seurcot,
Sy lui jure qu'il tendra pour l'escot.
Par les costez se prent ; « c'est Antecrist ! »
Crye, et jure par la mort Jhesucrist
Que non fera. Lors empoingne ung esclat,
Dessus son nez lui en faiz ung escript,
En ce bordeau où tenons nostre estat.

Puis paix se fait, et me fait ung groz pet,
Plus enffle qu'un velimeux escarbot.
Riant, m'assiet son poing sur mon sommet,
« Gogo » me dit, et me fiert le jambot.
Tous deux yvres dormons comme ung sabot.
Et au resveil, quant le ventre lui bruyt,
Monte sur moy, que ne gaste son fruyt.
Soubz elle geins, plus qu'un aiz me fait plat :
De paillarder tout elle me destruyt,
En ce bordeau où tenons nostre estat.

Ballade of Fat Margot

If here's the beauty that I gladly serve,
Must you then think that I'm a fool, a sot?
I'd take up shield and dagger for her love.
Name any charm you like, she has the lot.
When clients come, I run and grab a pot
Of wine (but softly softly, if you please!),
I bring them bread and water, fruit and cheese,
And if they pay up well, say "*Bene stat*:*
Next time you're randy, come and take your ease
Down in this whorehouse where we hold our court."   1600

Yet sometimes there's a most unholy row
When Margot comes to bed but brings no cash:
I just can't look at her, I loathe her now,
I seize her slip, her gown, her skirt, her sash,
And swear I'll get my cut from them. The clash
Hots up when Margot screams out "Antichrist!"
And, hands on hips, swears by the death of Christ
That she won't have it. Then I take a short
Plank and improve her nose (cheap at the price),
Down in this whorehouse where we hold our court.   1610

And then we make it up, she blasts me out
A fart whose stench would make dung beetles fly;
Laughing, she gives my head a hearty clout:
 "Gogo," says she, and slaps me on the thigh;
 Dead drunk, we sleep like logs, but by and by
 She wakes, because her belly starts to chide,
 And mounts me, not to hurt the fruit inside.
 Squashed flatter than a plank, I groan, I'm caught;
 She's knackered me for good with this last ride,
 Down in this whorehouse where we hold our court.   1620

129

Vente, gresle, gesle, j'ay mon pain cuyt.
Ie suis paillart, la paillarde me suyt.
Lequel vault mieulx ? Chacun bien s'entressuyt.
L'un vault l'autre : c'est à mau rat mau chat.
Ordure aimons, ordure nous affuyt ;
Nous deffuyons honneur, il nous deffuyt,
En ce bordeau où tenons nostre estat.

151 Item, à Marïon l'Idolle
Et la grant Jehanne de Bretaigne
Donne tenir publicque escolle
Où l'escollier le maistre enseigne.
Lieu n'est où ce merchié ne tiengne,
Synom à la grisle de Meun ;
De quoy je diz : « Fy de l'enseigne,
Puisque l'ouvraige es si commun ! »

152 Item, et à Noël Jolis,
Autre chose je ne lui donne
Fors plain poing d'oziers frez cueilliz
En mon jardin — je l'abandonne.
Chastoy est une belle aumosne,
Ame n'en doit estre marry :
Unze vings coups lui en ordonne,
Livrez par les mains de Henry.

153 Item, ne sçay qu'à l'Ostel Dieu
Donner, n'à povres hospitaulx.
Bourdes n'ont icy temps ne lieu,
Car povres gens ont assez maulx.
Chacun leur envoye leurs oz :
Les Mendïans ont eu mon oye ;
Au fort, ilz en auront les oz :
A menues gens, menue monnoye.

Vile rain, cold wind! So what? my bread comes free.
If I'm a lecher, lecher so is she.
Like sticks to like, and we're well matched, you see –
Like cat and rat, deep down the same bad sort.
Our filth we love, filth follows such as we;
Now honour's fled, and honour's what we flee
Down in this whorehouse where we hold our court.

151   Item: to Jeanne of Brittany
       And Idol Marion I give
       The rule of an academy   1630
       Where students educate the staff.
       There's no place where that school won't thrive,
       Except for Meung (that prison cell);
       Forget the sign! It's quite enough
       To know the trade is doing well.

152   Item: for Noël Jolis now,*
       I've nothing else to give him but
       A birch of willow twigs that grow
       In my own garden, freshly cut.
       Chastisement makes the soul more fit   1640
       For heaven, and no one should complain:
       Eleven score lashes he shall get:
       Laid on by Henry for more pain.

153   I don't know what to give the folk
       In hospices that house the poor.
       The Hôtel-Dieu's no place to joke:
       The poor have pains enough to endure.
       When hunger bites, scraps are the cure,
       And when the Mendicants pick bare
       My goose, they'll have the bones, for sure: 1650
       Small people get the smallest share.

154   Item, je donne à mon barbier
        Qui se nomme Colin Galerne,
        Près voisin d'Angelot l'herbier,
        Ung groz glaçon — prins où ? en Marne —,
        Afin qu'à son aise s'yverne.
        De l'estomac le tiengne près :
        Se l'iver ainsi se gouverne,
        Il aura chault l'esté d'après.

155   Item, riens aux Enffans Trouvés,
        Mais les perduz fault que consolle.
        Sy doivent estre retrouvez,
        Par droit sur Marïon l'Idolle.
        Une leçon de mon escolle
        Leur liray, qui ne dure guerre.
        Teste n'ayent dure ne folle :
        Escoutent ! car c'est la derniere.

Belle leçon aux enfants perdus

156   « Beaulx enfans, vous perdez la plus
        Belle roze de vo chappeau ;
        Mes clercs, près prenans comme glus,
        Se vous allez à Montpipeau
        Ou à Rüel, gardez la peau,
        Car, pour s'esbatre en ces deux lieux,
        Cuidant que vaulsist le rappeau,
        Le perdyt Colin de Cayeulx.

157   « Ce n'est pas ung jeu de troys mailles,
        Où va corps, et peult estre l'ame.
        Qui pert, riens n'y font repentailles
        C'on n'en meurre à honte et diffame ;
        Et qui gaigne n'a pas à femme
        Dido, la royne de Cartaige.
        L'omme est donc bien fol et infame
        Qui pour si peu couche tel gaige.

154   Item, my barber, whom you know
       Under the name Colin Galerne,
       Neighbour to herbalist Angelot,
       Gets a fresh block of ice from Marne.
       The winter won't seem quite so stern
       If he can hug it to his gut.
       He'll hibernate, and when the turn
       Of summer comes he'll feel quite hot.

155   Item: I'll give the Foundlings nowt: 1660
       The ones who need me are the Lost.
       But first, we'll need to find them out
       At Idol Marion's, I trust.
       My text's not long, but yet I must
       Read them this lesson from my school.
       So let them hear it: it's the last
       (Exit the thickhead and the fool).

                A Good Lesson for the Lost Boys

156   "My lovely lads, you may well lose
       The fairest rose your garlands bear;
       My studious clerks, if you should choose   1670
       To take your sticky claws elsewhere,
       Like Dicemont or Robbeville,* beware!
       By playing games in such a spot,
       Thinking one throw would make all square,
       Colin de Cayeux* lost the lot.

157   "It's not shove-ha'penny, this game,
       With body – maybe soul – at stake;
       Remorse won't save the loser from
       Disgraceful death for his mistake;
       As for the winner, he won't take   1680
       Away Queen Dido for his pains.
       The man's a bloody fool who stakes
       So much to make such petty gains.

158 « Q'un chacun encores m'escoute !
On dit — et il est verité —
Que charecterie se boit toute,
Au feu l'iver, au boys l'esté :
S'argent avez, il n'est quicté,
Mais le despendez tost et viste.
Qui en voyez vous herité ?
Jamaiz mal acquest ne prouffiite. »

Ballade de bonne doctrine

« Car, ou soies porteur de bulles,
Pipeur ou hazardeur de dez,
Tailleur de faulx coings, et te brulles
Comme ceulx qui sont eschaudez,
Traictres parjurs, de foy vuidez,
Soies laron, raviz ou pilles,
Où en va l'acquest, que cuidez ?
Tout aux tavernes et aux filles.

« Ryme, raille, cymballe, fluctes,
Comme folz fainctilz, eshontez ;
Farce, broulle, joue des fluctes,
Faiz es villes et es cytez
Farces, jeuz et moralitez ;
Gaigne au berlant, au glic, aux quilles,
Aussi bien va, or escoutez !
Tout aux tavernes et aux filles.

« De telz ordures te reculles ?
Labourre, faulches champs et prez,
Sers et penses chevaulx et mulles,
S'aucunement tu n'es lectrez ;
Assez araz, se prens en grez.
Mais, se chanvre broyes ou tilles,
Ne tens ton labour qu'as ouvrez
Tout aux tavernes et aux filles ?

158   "Now listen once again, and stay
To hear a proverb (and it's true):
The carter drinks his load away
All winter long and summer too:
The fireside or the woods will do.
Money? You'll blow the lot. And then
Who is your heir? Just tell me, who?   1690
No profit from ill-gotten gain."

Ballade of Good Doctrine

"For whether you're a pardoner,
A gambler with his loaded dice,
A perjurer who has no honour,
A forger whose false coinage buys
The oil in which his body fries,*
A pilferer with picky paws –
Where do you think the profit lies?
All with the taverns and the whores

"Rhyme, scoff, clash cymbals, pluck the lute,   1700
Like some cheap fool or shameless fraud;
Conjure, cajole with magic flute;
In town and cities tread the boards
With farce and interlude,* be lord
Of dice and cards; yet winning scores
Must surely go (now hear my words)
All to the taverns and the whores.

"You shrink from such disgusting courses?
Then seek the meadows, plough and mow,
Become a groom of mules and horses,   1710
If you're not one for books; and so
You'll still get by, just let it flow.
Try dressing hemp and other chores:
Where will those sweated wages go?
All to the taverns and the whores,

« Chausses, pourpoins esguilletez
Robes et toutes voz drappilles
Ains que vous fassiez piz, portez
Tout aux tavernes et aux filles !

159   « A vous parle, compains de galle,
        Qui estes de tous bons accors :
        Gardez vous tous de ce mau halle
        Qui noircist les gens quant sont mors ;
        Eschevez le : c'est ung mal mors.
        Passez vous au mieulx que pourrez,
        Et, pour Dieu, soiez tous recors :
        Une foyz viendra que mourrez. »

160   Item, je donne aux Quinze Vings
        (Qu'autant vauldroit nommer Troys Cens)
        De Paris, non pas de Prouvins,
        Car à ceulx tenu je me sens —
        Ilz auront, et je m'y consens,
        Sans les estuiz, mes grans lunectes,
        Pour mectre à part, aux Innocens,
        Les gens de bien des deshonnestes.

161   Icy n'y a ne riz ne jeu.
        Que leur valut avoir chevances
        N'en grans liz de paremens jeu,
        Engloutir vins, engrossir pances,
        Mener joyes, festes et dances,
        De ce fere prest à toute heure ?
        Toutes faillent telles plaisances,
        Et la coulpe si en demeure.

"Before you do much worse, I'd say:
Take your whole wardrobe – doublet, drawers,
Gown, shirt – and give the lot away,
All to the taverns and the whores.

159   "It's you I'm talking to, my mates   1720
In every jolly escapade:
Beware the blackening that awaits
The skin of people when they're dead;
Think of its mordant grasp with dread;
Stay clear; as best you can, get by.
For God's sake, get this in your heads:
The time will come when you shall die."

160   Item, the blind from Fifteen Twenties*
(Three Hundred if it pleases you),
Not of Provins, but Paris, meant as   1730
The ones that I'm beholden to –
They'll get (I reckon it's their due),
My largest specs without the case,
So, at the *Innocents** they'll know who
Was good or bad just by the face.

161   There's not much here to raise a laugh:
What good was all the wealth they'd got?
To lie in canopied beds, and quaff
Fine wines and feed a fatter gut,
With feasts and dances on the trot,   1740
Still ready to start up again?
All of such pleasures come to naught,
Only the guilt of them remains.

162   Quant je considere ces testes
Entassées en ces charniers,
Tous furent maistres des requestes,
Au moins de la Chambre aux Deniers,
Ou tous furent portepaniers ;
Autant puis l'un que l'autre dire,
Car d'evesques ou lanterniers
Je n'y congnois riens à reddire.

163   Et icelles qui s'enclinoient
Unes contres autres en leurs vies,
Desquelles les unes regnoient,
Des autres craintes et servies,
Là les voys toutes asouvies,
Ensemble en ung tas, pesle mesle ;
Seigneuries leur sont ravies,
Clerc ne maitre ne s'i appelle.

164   Or sont ilz mors, Dieu ait leurs ames !
Quant est des corps, ilz sont pourriz,
Aient esté seigneurs ou dames,
Souëf et tendrement nourriz
De cresme, froumentée ou riz,
Et les oz declinent en pouldre,
Ausquelz ne chault d'esbat ne riz.
Plaise au doulx Jhesus les assouldre !

165   Aux trespassez je faiz ce laiz
Et icelluy je communicque
A regens cours, sieges, palaiz,
Hayneurs d'avarice l'inicque,
Lesquelz pour la chose publicque
Se seichent les oz et les corps :
De Dieu et de saint Dominicque
Soïent absolz quant seront mors !

162   I think of all the skulls that lie
       Heaped up in every charnel house,
       Officials from the Treasury,
       On the king's payroll – can't be less:
       Or maybe pedlars at a guess;
       One or the other, don't ask me.
       Bishops or porters, take your choice: 1750
       No difference that I can see.

163   Some of those heads, while still alive,
       Would bow and bend to mighty men,
       Great lords who, born to rule and thrive,
       Were feared and served by others then.
       I see them lie, brought to their end,
       Together in a heap, pell-mell;
       No-one pulls rank, the names have gone
       Of clerk and master. Who could tell?

164   God keep their souls, for they are dead!   1760
       As for their bodies, now they rot,
       Though they were lords and ladies fed
       On fancy dishes cold and hot,
       Cream, rice and puddings from the pot;
       Their bones have crumbled into dust,
       Old lust and laughter stirs them not.
       Absolve them all, sweet Jesus Christ!

165   I leave the dead this legacy:
       And pass it on to the assize,
       To regent court and chancery,   1770
       Where men hate avarice and vice
       And for the common good devise
       To let their flesh and bones go dry:
       God and St Dominic the wise
       Absolve them when they come to die!

166 Item, riens à Jacquet Cardon,
  Car je n'ay rien pour lui d'onneste
  (Non pas que le gecte habandon)
  Synon ceste bergeronnecte ;
  S'elle eust le chant 'Marïonnecte',
  Fait pour Marïon la Peautarde,
  Ou d''Ouvrez vostre huys, Guillemecte',
  Elle alast bien à la moustarde.

Rondeau

  Au retour de dure prison,
  Où j'ay laissié presque la vie,
  Se Fortune a sur moy envie,
  Jugiez s'elle fait mesprison !
  Il me semble que par raison
  Elle eust bien estre assouvye
  Au retour.

  Se sy plaine est de desraison
  Que vueille que du tout desvie,
  Plaise à Dieu que l'ame ravye
  En soit lassus en sa maison
  Au retour !

167 Item, donne à maistre Lomer,
  Comme extraict que je suis de fée,
  Qu'il soit bien amé — mais d'amer
  Fille en chief ou femme coeffée,
  Ja n'en ayt la teste echauffée !
  Et qu'il ne ly couste une noix
  Faire ung soir cent foiz la faffée,
  En despit d'Auger le Danois.

166   Item: Jacquet Cardon whose merit
Suits nothing honest I could get;
But he's not one I'd disinherit,
So here's a rondeau. If it's set
To that sweet tune 'Marionette',   1780
An oldie that still hasn't rusted,
Or 'Open up there, Guillemette',
I reckon it would cut the mustard.

Rondeau

On my return from harsh and strong
Prison that almost cost my life,
If Fortune plagues me with such strife,
You judge if she be right or wrong.
It would be only right, I trust,
That, sated, she should grant relief
On my return.   1790

Yet if she's so unrighteous
To wish that I should die of grief,
May it please God that He receive
My soul above among the just
On my return!

167   Item, I grant Master Lomer,
(From fairy line this gift I claim)
To be beloved – he shouldn't care
To ask by whom: it's all the same,
Bare-headed lass or hatted dame;   1800
He'll shag a hundred times a night,
Not pay a bean, and put to shame
Bold Ogier, the Danish knight.

168   Item, donne aux amans enfermes,
        Oultre le laiz Alain Chartier,
        A leurs chevetz de pleurs et lermes
        Trestout fin plain ung benoistier,
        Et ung petit brain d'esglantier,
        En tous temps vert, pour guepillon,
        Pourveu qu'ilz diront le psaultier
        Pour l'ame du povre Villon.

169   Item, à maistre Jacques James,
        Qui se tue d'amasser biens,
        Donne fiancer tant de femmes
        Qu'il vouldra ; mais d'espouser, riens.
        Pour quy amasse il ? Pour les sciens ?
        Il ne plaint fors que ses morceaux ;
        Et qui fust aux truyes, je tiens
        Qu'il doit de droit estre aux pourceaux.

170   Item, le camus Seneschal,
        Qui uneffoys paia mes debtes,
        En recompence Mareschal
        Sera pour ferrer oyes, canectes,
        En luy envoyant ces sornectes
        Pour soy desennuyer ; combien,
        S'il veult, face en des alumectes :
        De beau chanter s'ennuyt on bien.

171   Item, au Chevalier du Guet
        Je donne deux beaux petiz paiges :
        Philebert et le groz Marcquet,
        Lesquelz servy, dont sont plus saiges,
        La plus partie de leurs aages
        Ont le prevost des mareschaulx.
        Helas ! s'ilz sont cassez de gaiges,
        Aler les fauldra tous deschaulx !

168   Item: to all the lovesick here,
Not just the story of their plight
By Chartier,* but a font of tears,
Brimful, beside their bed at night;
A sprig of eglantine upright,
With holy water in the bowl;
On one condition: they'll recite   1810
The Psalter for poor Villon's soul.

169   Item, to Master James, whose money
Is earned by toil that's never done,
The right to pledge his hand to many
Sweet girls, and not to marry one.
Who is he saving for? His kin?
He grudges his own meat and wine;
And yet, what once fed sows, I think,
Ought rightly to be food for swine.

170   Item: the snub-nosed Seneschal*   1820
Once paid my debts: for which I'll seize
This golden chance to make him marshal
His skills for shoeing ducks and geese:
To cheer him up I send him these
Trifles in verse, though with such rhymes
He can light fires if he please:
Fine singing gets too much at times.

171   Item: the Captain of the Watch*
Will get two handsome little pages,
Philbert and Fat Marcquet – a catch,   1830
Since both of them seem like old sages,
Because, when young, they served for ages
Under the Provost Marshall's rod.
If now they're sacked and have no wages,
Alas, they'll have to go unshod!

172   Item, à Chappelain je laisse
        Ma chappelle à simple tonsure,
        Chargée d'une seiche messe
        Où il ne fault grant lecture.
        Resiné lui eusse ma cure,
        Mais point ne veult de charge d'ames :
        De conffesser, ce dit, n'a cure
        Synon chamberieres et dames.

173   Pour ce que scet bien mon entente
        Jehan de Calais, honnorable homme,
        Qui ne me vist des ans a trente
        Et ne scet comment on me nomme,
        De tout ce testament, en somme,
        S'aucun y a difficulté,
        L'oster jusqu'au rez d'une pomme
        Je lui en donne faculté.

174   De le gloser et commenter,
        De le diffinir et descripre,
        Diminuer ou augmenter,
        De le canceller et prescripre
        De sa main (et ne sceut escripre),
        Interpreter et donner sens
        A son plaisir, meilleur ou pire —
        A tout cecy je m'y consens.

175   Et s'aucun, dont n'ay congnoissance,
        Estoit alé de mort à vie,
        Je vueil et lui donne puissance,
        Affin que l'ordre soit suyvie
        Pour estre mieulx parassouvye,
        Que ceste aulmosne ailleurs transporte,
        Car, s'il l'applicquoit par envye,
        A son ame je m'en rapporte.

172   Item: to Chapelain I pass
        My chapel (tonsure's all he'll need);
        Its only charge is one dry mass,*
        Which doesn't have too much to read:
        My parish, no – he wouldn't heed   1840
        The care of souls or hear confession;
        Although for dames in dire need
        And chambermaids he'd make exception.

173   Jean de Calais won't know my name,
        In thirty years we haven't met,
        And yet his honourable fame
        Fits him to judge this testament;
        I'm sure he knows just what I meant,
        So if some heirs should go to law,
        He has my firm and full consent   1850
        To peel this apple to the core.

174   To gloss it and to annotate,
        Give definition and description,
        To add things on or cut them out
        With cancellation and proscription;
        Though he's no scribe, it's his inscription,
        Interpreting and making sense,
        Better or worse – I've no objection,
        And all of it has my consent.

175   If, unbeknown to me, some heir   1860
        Has passed from death to life, I pray
        That my bequest should go elsewhere,
        And with this task I charge Calais;
        So that in the most proper way
        My will is done. But should his greed
        Take the gift for himself, I'd say:
        Let his own conscience judge the deed.

176 Item, j'ordonne à Saincte Avoye,
  Et non ailleurs, ma sepulture ;
  Et, afin q'un chascun me voye,
  Non pas en char, mais en painture,
  Que l'en tire mon estature
  D'encre, s'il ne coustoit trop cher.
  De tombel ? Riens ! Je n'en ay cure,
  Car il greveroit le plancher.

177 Item, vueil qu'autour de ma fosse
  Ce qui s'enssuit, sans autre histoire,
  Soit escript en lectre assez grosse ;
  Qui n'auroit point d'escriptouoire,
  De charbon ou de pierre noire,
  Sans en rien entamer le plastre.
  Au moins sera de moy memoire
  Telle qu'elle est d'un bon follastre.

EPITAPHE

178 Cy gist et dort en ce sollier
  Qu'Amours occist de son raillon,
  Ung povre petit escollier
  Qui fut nommé François Villon ;
  Oncques de terre n'eust sillon.
  Il donna tout, chacun le scet,
  Table, tresteaux, pain, corbillon.
  Pour Dieu, dictes en ce verset :

VERSET

  Repoz eternel donne à cil,
  Sire, et clarté perpetuelle,
  Qui vaillant plat ne escüelle
  N'eust oncques n'ung brain de percil.
  Il fut rez, chief, barbe, sourcil,
  Comme ung navet qu'on ret ou pelle :
  Repoz eternel donne à cil.

176   Item, I'd have my burial
At Sainte-Avoie* and not elsewhere;
I hope I shall be seen by all,   1870
Not in the flesh, but painted there.
A full-length portrait I'd prefer –
In ink, if it won't cost much more.
A tomb? No, nothing! I don't care;
It just might overload the floor.

177   Item, I will that at my grave
These words and nothing more be set,
Written in letters big and brave.
If writing tools are hard to get,
You can use coal or charcoal; but   1880
Don't scratch the plaster – that's a rule.
At least men will remember what
I was – a decent kind of fool.

EPITAPH

178   HERE SLEEPS IN THIS HIGH ROOM APART
A HUMBLE STUDENT ALL ALONE,
SLAIN EARLY BY LOVE'S MORTAL DART,
AS FRANÇOIS VILLON HE WAS KNOWN.
HE HAD NO LAND TO CALL HIS OWN,
AND WHAT HE HAD HE GAVE AWAY:
CHAIR, TABLE, BASKET, BREAD, ALL GONE.   1890
IN GOD'S NAME SAY THIS VERSE, I PRAY:

THE VERSE

GRANT HIM ETERNAL REST, O LORD,
AND SHINE WITH YOUR PERPETUAL LIGHT;
HE HAD NO CASH FOR BOWL OR PLATE,
AND PARSLEY HE COULD NOT AFFORD.
THEY SHAVED HIM CLOSE,* HEAD, BROW AND BEARD,
JUST LIKE A TURNIP, SCRAPED ALL WHITE.
GRANT HIM ETERNAL REST, O LORD.

RIGUEUR LE TRANSMIST EN EXIL
ET LUI FRAPPA AU CUL LA PELLE,
NON OBSTANT QU'IL DIT. « J'EN APPELLE »,
QUI N'EST PAS TERME TROP SUBTIL.
REPOZ ETERNEL DONNE À CIL.

179   Item, je vueil qu'on sonne à bransle
Le groz beffroy qui est de voirre,
Combien qu'il n'est cueur qui ne tremble,
Quant de sonner est à son erre.
Sauvé a mainte belle terre,
Le temps passé, chacun le scet :
Feussent gens d'armes ou tonnoire,
Au son de luy, tout mal cessoit.

180   Les sonneurs auront quatre miches
Et, se c'est peu, demye douzaine
(Autant n'en donnent les plus riches !)
Mais ilz seront de saint Estienne.
Volant est homme de grant peine :
L'un en sera ; quant g'y regarde,
Il en vivra une sepmainne.
Et l'autre ? Auffort, Jehan de la Garde.

181   Pour tout ce fournir et parfaire,
J'ordonne mes executeurs,
Ausquelz fait bon avoir affaire
Et contentent bien leur debteurs.
Ilz ne sont pas moult grans vanteurs
Et ont bien de quoy, Dieu mercys !
De ce fait seront directeurs.
Escryptz : je t'en nommeray six.

His arse got belted with a spade
When prison was his cruel fate;
Though he said "I appeal", he might
Have chosen a more subtle word.
Grant him eternal rest, O Lord.

1900

179   Item, let the Glass Bell send out
       A mighty peal that's loud and long,
       Although there is no heart so stout
       As not to tremble when it's rung.
       As all men know, its warning tongue
       Saved many a fine land for peace,
       Though storms might threaten, bandits throng,   1910
       The bell made all such evils cease.

180   The bell-ringers will get four loaves.
       Not much, you say? then half a dozen,
       (It's more than any rich man gives!)
       Like buns they hand out on St Stephen's.
       First ringer is Volant, I reckon,
       Because he works so very hard,
       A bun lasts him a week. The second...
       Well, let me think... Jean de la Garde.

181   To see it done all fair and square,   1920
       I name executors; they're just
       The types you need for such affairs,
       And men their creditors can trust.
       They're far from showy, but they must
       Have quite enough to call their own,
       Thank God. Here's six upon the list
       Of my directors: write it down.

182   C'est maistre Mertin Bellefoye,
       Lieutenant du cas criminel.
       Qui sera l'autre ? G'y pensoye :
       Ce sera sire Colombel ;
       S'il lui plaist et il lui est bel,
       Il entreprendra ceste charge.
       Et l'autre ? Michiel Juvenel.
       Ces troys seulz et pour tout j'en charge.

183   Mais, ou cas qu'ilz s'en excusassent
       En redoubtant les premiers fraiz,
       Ou totalement reffusassent,
       Ceulx qui s'enssuivent cy après
       Institue, gens de bien très :
       Phelippe Bruneau, noble escuier,
       Et l'autre ? Son voisin d'emprès :
       Sy est maistre Jacques Raiguier.

184   Et l'autre ? Maistre Jacques James :
       Troys hommes de bien et d'onneur,
       Desirans de sauver leurs ames
       Et doubtans Dieu Nostre Seigneur.
       Plus tost y mecteront du leur
       Que ceste ordonnance ne baillent ;
       Point n'auront de contreroleur,
       Mais à leur seul plaisir en taillent.

185   Des testamens qu'on dit le Maistre
       De mon fait n'arra quy ne *quot*,
       Mais ce fera ung jeune prestre
       Qui est nommé Thomas Tricquot.
       Voulentiers busse à son escot,
       Et qu'il me coutast ma cornecte !
       S'il sceust jouer en ung tryppot,
       Il eust de moy le *Trou Perrecte*.

182   First I'll have Martin Bellefaye,
Lieutenant of the Criminal Court,
As for the next? What would you say   1930
To Colombel? That's what I thought.
He'll take it if it is the sort
Of job he likes, he'll get it done.
The third is Juvenel. In short,
These are the three I'm counting on.

183   But if they seek some vague excuse
Because of the initial cost,
Or if they totally refuse,
I've got three more, among the best
That can be had – and here's the list.   1940
Philippe Brunel,* a noble squire,
And Master Raguier, his most
Near neighbour in the same old choir.

184   Master Jacques James rounds off the roll –
Three men of honour and repute,
Who duly seek to save their souls,
And turn to God the Lord in doubt.
Rather than fail to carry out
This will, they'll all chip in, no fear.
Be sure they'll cut the cloth to suit   1950
Themselves without an overseer.

185   The so-called Master of the Wills
Won't make from me a *quid ne quod*;
Young Tom Tricquot the priest fulfils
All the conditions, gets the nod.
I'd drink at his expense, by God,
And lose my hatband or my soul! –
If he played on my court, the lad
Would soon be offered *Perrette's Hole*.*

186   Quant au regard du luminaire,
Guillaume du Ru j'y commectz.
Pour porter les coings du suaire,
Aux executeurs le remectz.
Trop plus me font mal c'oncques maiz
Barbe, cheveux, penil, sourcys.
Mal me presse, temps desormaiz
Que crye à toutes gens mercys.

Ballade de merci

A Chartreux et à Celestins,
A Mendïans et à Devoctes,
A musars et clacquepatins,
A servans et filles mignoctes
Portans seurcoz et justes coctes,
A cuidereaux d'amours transsiz
Chauçans sans mehain fauves boctes —
Je crye à toutes gens mercys.

A fillectes monstrans tetins
Pour avoir plus largement hostes,
A ribleurs, menneurs de hutins,
A batelleurs traynans mermoctes,
A folz, folles, à sotz, à soctes,
Qui s'en vont cyfflant six à six
A vecyes et marïoctes, —
Je crye à toutes gens mercys.

Synon aux traitres chiens matins
Qui m'ont fait ronger dures crostes,
Macher mains soirs et mains matins,
Que ores je ne crains troys croctes.
Je feisse pour eulx pez et roctes —
Je ne puis, car je suis assiz.
Auffort, pour esviter rïoctes,
Je crye à toutes gens mercys.

Guillaume du Ru, I trust, will guide   1960
The lamps that lead my funeral.
I'll let the executors decide
Who should be bearers of my pall.
My head, my brow, my beard, my balls,
Everything pains me more and more.
The time has come, the moment calls,
Of all men pardon to implore

Ballade of Pardon

Of Chartreux and of Celestines,
Of friars, nuns of good repute,
Of idlers who clack heels and preen,   1970
Of pimps, and whores who stuff their cute
Bodies in bodices too tight,
Of fops who faint and fight love's war,
Easy in fancy fawn high boots –
Of all men pardon I implore.

Of girls with gowns that show their tits
To keep more clients on the go,
Of petty thieves and brawling twits,
Of mountebanks with apes in tow,
Of fools and sots, six in a row,   1980
Who march and whistle till they're sore,
With baubles, cap and bells on show –
Of all men pardon I implore.

Except for the vile dogs who made
Me gnaw hard crusts each eve and morn;
Three turds would make me more afraid,
I'd belch and fart for every one –
But now, because I'm sitting on
My deathbed, cannot any more.
Still, to end quarrels and have done,   1990
Of all men pardon I implore.

C'on leur froisse les quinze costes
De groz mailletz, fors et massiz,
De plombées et telz peloctes !
Je crye à toutes gens mercys.

Ballade de conclusion

Icy se clost le testament
Et finist du povre Villon.
Venez à son enterrement,
Quant vous orez le carrillon,
Vestuz rouge com vermeillon,
Car en amours mourut martir :
Ce jura il sur son coullon,
Quant de ce monde voult partir.

Et je croy bien que pas n'en ment,
Car chassié fut comme ung soullon
De ses amours hayneusement,
Tant que d'icy à Roussillon
Brosses n'y a ne brossillon
Qui n'eust, ce dit il sans mentir,
Ung lambeau de son cotillon,
Quant de ce monde voult partir.

Il est ainsi et tellement :
Quant mourut, n'avoit qu'un haillon.
Qui plus, en mourant mallement
L'espoignoit d'Amours l'esguillon ;
Plus agu que le ranguillon
D'un baudrier lui faisoit sentir
(C'est de quoy nous esmerveillon)
Quant de ce monde voult partir.

Prince, gent comme esmerillon,
Saichiez qu'il fist au departir :
Ung tract but de vin morillon,
Quant de ce monde voult partir.

May someone smash their fifteen ribs
With massive heavy mallets or
Lead cannonballs and suchlike squibs!
Of all men pardon I implore.

Ballade to Conclude

Here ends the will and testament
Of poor Villon, his end as well.
Come to his burial and attend
When you shall hear the solemn bell;
Put on your scarlet robe to tell   2000
He died love's martyr, for he signed
And swore it by his one good ball
Just as he left this world behind.

And I believe he told no lie,
For he was hounded by the pack
Far from his loves and forced to flee;
From here to Roussillon the track
Has not a bramble, brier or brake,
He truly said, where you won't find
Shreds of his coat, torn from his back   2010
Just as he left this world behind.

That's how it was, and when he died
He died in rags. What's more, the strong
Sharp spur of love still pricked his hide;
Dying, he felt that rising pang;
Worse than a baldric's buckle-tongue
That cut was then the most unkind
(And here's what sets us wondering)
Just as he left this world behind.

Prince of the merlin's noble line,   2020
Hear what he did as he resigned;
He took one swig of dark red wine
Just as he left this world behind.

155

Miscellaneous Poems

(*Poésies diverses*)

I – Ballade des proverbes

Tant grate chievre que mau gist ;
Tant va le pot à l'eaue qu'il brise ;
Tant chauf'on le fer qu'il rougist,
Tant le maill'on qu'il se debrise ;
Tant vault l'omme comme on le prise,
Tant s'eslongne il qu'il n'en souvient,
Tant mauvais est qu'on le desprise ;
Tant crie l'on Noël qu'il vient.

Tant parl'on qu'on se contredit ;
Tant vault bon bruyt que grace acquise ;
Tant promest on qu'on se desdit ;
Tant pri'on que chose est acquise,
Tant plus est chere et plus est quise,
Tant la quiert on qu'on y parvient,
Tant plus commune, et mains requise ;
Tant crye l'on Noël qu'il vient.

Tant ayme on chien qu'on le nourrist ;
Tant court chanson qu'elle est aprise ;
Tant gard'on fruit qu'il se pourrist ;
Tant bat on place qu'elle est prise ;
Tant tarde on que fault entreprise ;
Tant se haste on que mal advient ;
Tant embrasse on que chiet la prise ;
Tant crye l'on Noël qu'il vient.

Tant raille on que plus on n'en rit ;
Tant despend on qu'on n'a chemise ;
Tant est on franc que tout s'i frit ;
Tant vault « tien » que chose promise ;
Tant ayme on Dieu qu'on suyt l'Eglise ;
Tant donne on qu'emprunter convient ;
Tant tourne vent qu'il chiet en bise ;
Tant crye l'on Noël qu'il vient.

I – Ballade of Proverbs*

The more the goat scratches, the less well she lies;
The more the pot's filled, the more surely it cracks;
The more iron's heated, the brighter it glows,
The more that it's worked on, the sooner it breaks;
The more a man's worthy, the more he is praised,
The more he's away, the less spoken his name,
The more he seeks evil, the more he's despised;
The more you cry "Christmas", the sooner it comes.

The more a man chatters, the less sense he makes;
The more fame he acquires, more favour he'll meet;   10
The more that he pledges, the more oaths he breaks;
The more you keep asking, more surely you'll get,
The more something's costly, the more it is sought,
The more common it may be, the lesser its charm.
The more you go seeking, the sooner you'll find;
The more you cry "Christmas", the sooner it comes.

The more a song's heard, the less it's forgotten:
The more a dog's loved, the more often it's fed;
The more a fruit's kept, the more surely it's rotten;
The more a fort's battered, the sooner it falls;   20
The more you delay, the more plans will collapse;
The more you make haste, the more hopes are undone;
The more you embrace, the less matter you clasp;
The more you cry "Christmas", the sooner it comes.

The more you keep joking, the less men will laugh;
The more a man spends, the more tattered his shirt;
The more that is promised proves less than enough;
The more you're free-handed, the more you go short;
The more that you give, the more cash you must borrow;
The more God is loved, the more churches are crammed: 30
The more the wind turns, the more cold is tomorrow;
The more you cry "Christmas", the sooner it comes.

Prince, tant vit fol qu'il s'avise
Tant va il qu'après il revient,
Tant le mate on qu'il se ravise.
Tant crye l'on Noël qu'il vient.

The more a fool lives, Prince, the more he will learn,
The more that he travels, the sooner he's home,
The more he gets beaten, the wiser he'll turn;
The more you cry "Christmas", the sooner it comes.

II – Ballade des menus propos

Je congnois bien mousches en laict,
Je congnois à la robe l'homme,
Je congnois le beau temps du lait,
Je congnois au pommier la pomme,
Je congnois l'arbre à veoir la gomme,
Je congnois quant tout est de mesmes,
Je congnois qui besoigne ou chomme :
Je congnois tout fors que moy mesmes.

Je congnois pourpoint au colet
Je congnois le moyne à la gonne,
Je congnois le maistre au varlet,
Je congnois au voile la nonne,
Je congnois quant pipeur gergonne,
Je congnois fols nourris de cresmes,
Je congnois le vin à la tonne :
Je congnois tout fors que moy mesmes.

Je congnois cheval et mulet,
Je congnois leur charge et leur somme,
Je congnois Bietrix et Belet,
Je congnois gect qui nombre assomme,
Je congnois visïon et somme,
Je congnois la faulte des Boesmes,
Je congnois le povoir de Romme :
Je congnois tout fors que moy mesmes.

Prince, je congnois tout en somme,
Je congnois colorez et blesmes,
Je congnois Mort qui tout consomme :
Je congnois tout fors que moy mesmes.

II – Ballade of Trivial Things

I know a man by what he wears,
I know the milk that drowns the fly,
I know foul weather isn't fair,
I know the apple by its tree,
I know the tree by sap that oozes,
I know when all's the same to me,
I know who's working and who snoozes,
I know all things except myself.

I know the collar proves the jacket
I know the master by his man,   10
I know the monk is made by habit,
I know the veil reveals the nun,
I know how sharpers gab and quarrel,
I know that cream feeds foolish men,
I know the best wine by the barrel,
I know all things except myself.

I know the horse, the mule as well,
I know the burden that they carry,
I know both Beatrice and Belle,
I know the beads that mark the tally,   20
I know the vision and the dream,
I know the Hussite heresy*,
I know the power that's in Rome,
I know all things except myself.

My Prince, I know how things befall.
I know pale sickness, glowing health,
I know Death who devours all,
I know all things except myself.

III – *Ballade des contre-vérités*

Il n'est soing que quant on a fain,
Ne service que d'ennemy,
Ne mascher qu'ung botel de faing,
Ne fort guet que de homme endormy,
Ne clemence que felonnie,
N'asseurence que de peureux,
Ne foy que de homme qui regnye,
Ne bien conseillé que amoureux.

Il n'est engendrement qu'en boing,
Ne bon bruit que de homme benny,
Ne riz qu'après ung cop de poing,
Ne lotz que debtes mectre en ny,
Ne vraye amour qu'en flaterye,
N'encontre que de maleureux,
Ne vray rapport que menterye,
Ne bien conseillé que amoureux.

Ne tel repos que vivre en soing,
N'oneur porter que dire « Fy ! »
Ne soy vanter que de faulx coing,
Ne santé que de homme bouffy,
Ne hault vouloir que couardye,
Ne conseil que de furïeulx,
Ne doulceur qu'en femme estourdye,
Ne bien conseillé que amoureux.

Voulez vous que verté vous dye ?
Il n'est jouer qu'en maladie,
Letre vraye que tragedye,
Lasches homs que chevalereux,
Orrible son que melodye,
Ne bien conseillé que amoureux.

III – Ballade of Contradictions

There's no great care but going hungry,
Nor food to chew but bales of hay,
Nor help but from an enemy,
Nor guard but one who sleeps all day,
Nor kindness that's not cruelty,
Nor peace of mind not scared of life,
Nor faith that doesn't faith deny,
Nor wise man who is not in love.

There's no conceiving but in baths,*
Nor exile without fair repute,   10
Nor clout that doesn't raise a laugh,
Nor praise but for an unpaid debt,
No true love but in flattering suit,
Nor cheer but what poor wretches give,
Nor, without lies, a true report,
Nor wise man who is not in love.

Nor any rest like anxious life,
Nor boast but of some counterfeit,
Nor compliment like "Bugger off",
Nor health but in a swollen gut,   20
Nor courage but where cowards sweat,
Nor reason but where madmen rave,
Nor sweetness but in shrewish spite,
Nor wise man who is not in love.

Vain words? Then here's the truth for you:
In sickness only there's some fun,
Lying old fables tell what's true,
Low cowards are our knights most brave;
One finds no discord but in tune,
Nor wise man who is not in love.   30

IV *Ballade du concours de Blois*

Je meurs de seuf auprès de la fontaine,
Chault comme feu, et tremble dent à dent ;
En mon pays suis en terre loingtaine ;
Lez ung brasier frissonne tout ardent,
Nu comme ung ver, vestu en president ;
Je riz en pleurs et attens sans espoir ;
Confort reprens en triste desespoir :
Je m'esjouÿs et n'ay plaisir aucun ;
Puissant je suis sans force et sans pouoir,
Bien recueully, debouté de chascun.

Rien ne m'est seur que la chose incertaine,
Obscur fors ce qui est tout evident ;
Doubte ne fais fors en chose certaine ;
Scïence tiens à soudain accident,
Je gaigne tout et demeure perdent ;
Au point du jour diz : « Dieu vous doint bon soir ! »
Gisant envers, j'ay grant paeur de chëoir ;
J'ay bien de quoy, et si n'en ay pas ung ;
Echoicte actens et d'omme ne suis hoir,
Bien recueully, debouté de chascun.

De riens n'ay soing, si mectz toute m'atayne
D'acquerir biens, et n'y suis pretendant ;
Qui mieulx me dit, c'est cil qui plus m'actaine,
Et qui plus vray, lors plus me vas bourdent ;
Mon ami est qui me faict entendent
D'un cigne blanc que c'est un corbeau noir,
Et qui me nuyst, croy qu'i m'ayde à pourvoir ;
Bourde, verté au jour d'uy m'est tout ung ;
Je retiens tout, rien ne sçay concepvoir,
Bien recueully, debouté de chascun.

IV *Ballade from the Contest at Blois**

I die of thirst here where the fountain flows,
As hot as fire, yet with chattering teeth;
I'm in some distant land and home is close;
The brazier makes me shiver with its heat;
Dressed like a judge and stripped from head to foot,
I laugh in tears and hopeless linger on;
Comfort I find in sad despair again;
Still I rejoice and yet I have no joy;
Power is mine while strength and force have gone,
Made welcome, and by all men turned away.   10

What's most uncertain reassures me most,
Nothing's obscure but what is brought to light;
Knowledge is a mere accident that grows
From sudden chance; what's certain makes me doubt;
Always a winner, yet I still lose out;
I say "Good night to all" when day comes on;
I'm scared of falling while I'm lying down;
I'm flush and broke, expect a legacy
Although I'm not the heir to anyone,
Made welcome, and by all men turned away.   20

I care for nothing, all my effort goes
On getting goods to which I have no right;
The man who speaks me fair offends me most,
The biggest liar brings me truth and light,
That man's my friend who makes me think a white
Bird is pitch-black, a crow and not a swan;
I think that those who harm me help me on;
Lies or the truth – they seem all one today;
My memory's perfect; but ideas? Not one;
Made welcome, and by all men turned away.   30

Prince clement, or vous plaise sçavoir
Que j'entens moult et n'ay sens ne sçavoir ;
Parcïal suis, à toutes loys commun.
Que fais je plus ? Quoy ! Les gaiges ravoir,
Bien recueully, debouté de chascun.

Noble and gracious Prince, be pleased to learn
I have sharp wits, but sense and learning none;
I'm factious, yet in general I obey;
What else? I'd take my pledges back again;
Made welcome, and by all men turned away.

V – *Louange à Marie d'Orléans*

Jam nova progenies celo demittitur alto

1   O louée concepcïon
       Envoiée sa jus des cieulx,
       Du noble lis digne sÿon,
       Don de Jhesus très precïeulx,
       Marie, nom très gracïeulx,
       Fons de pitié, source de grace,
       La joye, confort de mes yeulx,
       Qui nostre paix batist et brasse !

2   La paix : c'est assavoir des riches,
       Des povres le substantement,
       Le rebours des felons et chiches.
       Très necessaire enfantement,
       Conceu, porté honnestement
       — Hors le pechié originel —
       Que dire je puis sainctement
       Souverain bien de Dieu eternel.

3   Nom recouvré, joye de peuple,
       Confort des bons, des maulx retraicte,
       Du doulx seigneur premiere et seule
       Fille de son cler sang extraicte,
       Du dextre costé Clovis traicte,
       Glorïeuse ymage en tous fais,
       Ou hault ciel créée et pourtraicte
       Pour esjouyr et donner paix.

4   En l'amour et crainte de Dieu
       Es nobles flans Cesar conceue
       Des petis et grans en tout lieu
       A très grande joye receue,
       De l'amour Dieu traicte et issue

V – In Praise of Marie d'Orléans

*Iam nova progenies cælo demittitur alto**

1   Purest Conception, praise be thine,
To earth descended from the skies,
The noble lily's flower divine,
Most precious gift of Jesus Christ,
Mary, a name beyond all price,
Fountain of pity, source of grace,
The joy, the solace of my eyes,
Who makes and then maintains our peace!

2   Peace that gives rich men wealth, I mean,
And sustenance to the poor and lowly,   10
Hostile to all that's foul and mean;
Most necessary birth and holy,
Conceived immaculate and wholly
Preserved from man's original stain,
Chief good – and this I say most truly –
Of the eternal God who reigns.

3   Name found again, the joy of man,
Refuge and solace of the good,
A daughter, first and only one
Of our dear lord's illustrious blood,   20
Drawn from old Clovis's right side,*
The glorious figure and device
That heaven creates when it decides
To make us all rejoice in peace.

4   In love and fear of God the Lord,
Through Caesar's noble loins conceived,
By great and small with one accord
And overwhelming joy received,
By God's love fashioned and achieved

Pour les discordez ralïer
Et aux encloz donner yssue,
Leur lïans et fers deslïer.

5   Aucunes gens, qui bien peu sentent,
       Nourriz en simplesse et confiz,
       Contre le vouloir Dieu attentent,
       Par ignorance desconfiz,
       Desirans que feussiez ung filz ;
       Mais qu'ainsy soit, ainsy m'aist Dieux,
       Je croy que ce soit grant proufiz.
       Raison : Dieu fait tout pour le mieux.

6   Du Psalmiste je prens les dictz :
       Delectasti me, Domine,
       In factura tua ; si diz :
       Noble enfant, de bonne heure né,
       A toute doulceur destiné,
       Manna du ciel, celeste don,
       De tout bienfait le guerdonné
       Et de noz maulx le vray pardon.

                    Double Ballade

       Combien que j'ay leu en ung dit :
       Inimicum putes, y a,
       Qui te presentem laudabit,
       Toutesfois, non obstant cela,
       Oncques vray homme ne cela
       En son courage aucun grant bien
       Qui ne le monstrast çà et là :
       On doit dire du bien le bien.

       Saint Jehan Baptiste ainsy le fist
       Quant l'Aignel de Dieu descela ;
       En ce faisant pas ne mesfist,

To come and make all factions cease,   30
To see all prisoners reprieved,
From chains and fetters grant release.

5   Some folk who have but little sense,
Unlearned simple-minded men,
Defy God's will through ignorance,
And thus they find themselves undone,
By wishing you had been a son.
Let this be as it is: we're blest,
(God help me!) with great things to come,
For God does all things for the best.   40

6   I follow where the Psalmist led;
Delectasti me, Domine,
In factura tua,* so he said,
And I repeat: sweet destiny,
Child born upon a happy day,
Manna celestial, gift from Heaven,
Reward for all good deeds, true way
By which our sins will be forgiven.

Double Ballade

In some old text I know a bit
Inimicum putes, I read   50
Qui te presentem laudabit;*
And yet, in spite of what it said,
No good man ever sought to hide
Some good within his heart; he would
Rather proclaim it far and wide;
One must speak well of what is good.

That's how the Baptist handled it
When he revealed the Lamb of God;
He wasn't wrong when he saw fit

Dont sa voix es tourbes vola,
De quoy saint Andry Dieu loua,
Qui de lui cy ne sçavoit rien,
Et au Filz de Dieu s'aloua :
On doit dire du bien le bien.

Envoiée de Jhesucrist
Rappeller sa jus par deça
Les povres que Rigueur proscript
Et que Fortune betourna,
Cy sçay bien comment y m'en va :
De Dieu, de vous vie je tien.
Benoist celle qui vous porta !
On doit dire du bien le bien.

Cy devant Dieu fais congnoissance
Que creature feusse morte,
Ne feust vostre doulce naissance,
En charité puissant et forte,
Qui ressuscite et reconforte
Ce que Mort avoit prins pour sien.
Vostre presence me conforte.
On doit dire du bien le bien.

Cy vous rans toute obeÿssance
Ad ce faire Raison m'exorte,
De toute ma povre puissance.
Plus n'est deul qui me desconforte
N'aultre ennuy de quelconque sorte :
Vostre je suis et non plus mien.
Ad ce Droit et Devoir m'enhorte :
On doit dire du bien le bien.

O grace et pitié tres immense,
L'entrée de paix et la porte,
Some de benigne clemence,
Qui noz faultes toust et supporte

To raise his voice above the crowd.   60
And then St Andrew praised the Lord,
Serving God's son just as he should,
Who till that day knew not the Word:
One must speak well of what is good.

Envoy of Jesus Christ sent out
To call and gather to His side
The poor whom cruel Fortune flouts
And Justice threatens in its pride.
I know myself I must have died:
I owe my life to you and God;   70
Blest be the womb where you abode!
One must speak well of what is good.

Now before God, I make it clear
That I was very like to die
Had your sweet birth not saved me here
In potent perfect charity,
Which first revives and then sets free
What Death had seized and set aside
As his. Your presence comforts me:
One must speak well of what is good.   80

My full obedience I swear
To you – as Reason urges me –
With all my strength, with all my care.
I fear no grief or misery
Of any kind: yours I must be,
No more my own. This be this guide,
Here Right and Duty both agree:
One must speak well of what is good.

O grace and pity vast and clear,
The door of peace and mercy's key,   90
Forgiving faults we poor men share,
Essence indeed of clemency,

Se de vous louer me deporte,
Ingrat suis, et je le maintien,
Dont en ce refrain me transporte :
On doit dire du bien le bien.

Princesse, ce loz je vous porte
Que sans vous je ne feusse rien ;
A vous et à tous m'en rapporte :
On doit dire du bien le bien.

7 Euvre de Dieu, digne, louée
   Autant que nulle creature,
   De tous biens et vertus douée
   — Tant d'esperit que de nature,
   Que de ceulx qu'on dit d'aventure —
   Plus que rubis noble ou balais :
   Selon de Caton l'escripture :
   Patrem insequitur proles.

8 Port asseuré, maintien rassiz
   Plus que ne peut nature humaine,
   Et eussiez des ans trente-six ;
   Enfance en rien ne vous demaine.
   Que jour ne le die et sepmaine
   Je ne sçay qui le me deffant.
   Ad ce propoz ung dit ramaine :
   De saige mere saige enfant.

9 Dont resume ce que j'ay dit :
   Nova progenies celo,
   Car c'est du poete le dit,
   Jamjam demittitur alto.
   Saige Cassandre, bele Echo,
   Digne Judich, caste Lucresse,
   Je vous congnois, noble Dido,
   A ma seule dame et maistresse.

If I cease praising you, then I
Am thankless, be it understood;
So my refrain must ever be:
One must speak well of what is good.

Without you I am nothing; may
I praise you, Princess, as I should.
To you and all men, let me say:
One must speak well of what is good.   100

7   Praiseworthy work of God, endowed
Far more than any other creature
With every virtue, every good –
Gifts of the mind and character
No less than those of Fortune's favour –
More rare than rubies. Cato says,
Thinking of such a noble nature:
*Patrem insequitur proles.**

8   A noble mien, an air more steady
Than human nature could attain   110
If you were thirty-six already;
So far you are from childhood's reign.
No man can hinder my refrain,
Day in, day out my voice shall rise.
The proverb makes it very plain:
Wise mother bears a child that's wise.

9   Let me repeat what I have said,
Nova progenies cælo
(It's in the poet that I read)
Iamiam demittitur alto.   120
Cassandra wise and fair Echo,
Brave Judith and Lucrece the chaste
And noble Dido – these I know
In my sole lady's sovereign grace.

10   Et priant Dieu, digne pucelle,
      Qu'i vous doint longue et bonne vie
      — Qui vous ayme, ma demoiselle,
      Ja ne coure sur lui envie ! —
      Entiere dame et assouvie,
      J'espoir de vous servir ainçoys,
      Certes, se Dieu plaist, que devie
      Vostre povre escolier Françoys.

10   Most worthy maid, to God I pray
      That long and happy life be yours,
      And that whoever loves you may
      Meet with no envy in his course;
      Perfected lady, all my force
      Is bent to serve you with my whole   130
      Life until God shall take the soul
      Of this poor scholar, your François.

VI – Requête au Prince

Le mien seigneur et prince redoubté,
Floron de lis, roialle geniture,
Françoys Villon, que Travail a dompté
A coups orbes, à force de batture,
Vous supplie par ceste humble escripture
Que luy faciez quelque gracïeux prest.
De s'obliger en toutes cours est prest,
Se doubte avés que bien ne vous contante :
Sans y avoir dommage n'interest,
Vous n'y perdrés seulement que l'attente.

De prince n'a ung denier empruncté,
Fors de vous seul, vostre humble creature.
De six escuz que luy avés presté,
Lesquelx il mist pieça en nourriture,
Tout ce paiera ensemble, c'est droiture ;
Mais ce sera legierement et prest,
Car se de glan rancontre la forest
D'entour Pactay et chastaignes ont vente,
Paié vous tient sans delay ny arrest :
Vous n'y perdrés seulement que l'attente.

Si je povoie vendre de ma santé
A ung Lombart, usurier par nature,
Faulte d'argent m'a si fort enchanté
Que j'en prendroie, ce croy bien, l'avanture.
Argent ne pend à gipon n'à saincture.
Biau Sire Dieu ! je m'esbahis que c'est,
Car devant moy croix ne se comparest,
Sinon de bois ou pierre, que ne mente ;
Mais s'une foiz la vraye s'apparest,
Vous n'y perdrés seulement que l'attente.

VI – Request to the Prince*

My noble lord and most redoubted prince,
A fleur-de-lys, born of the royal line,
François Villon, worn out at last by dint
Of suffering, beatings, blows of every kind,
Begs of you, in this letter's humble lines,
A gracious loan to ease his misery.
If you should have the slightest doubt that he
Will pay you back, he'll swear in any court
Not to default on interest or fee;
You will lose nothing but the time you wait.   10

Your humble servant never took a penny
From any other prince, that's understood;
As for the six *écus* you lent already,
Some time ago he turned them into food:
He'll pay both debts together, as he should –
And soon! For if he gathers on his way
Some chestnuts in the woods around Pactay,*
He'll find they sell at a tremendous rate.
With that he'll have you paid without delay:
You will lose nothing but the time you wait.   20

It's health that counts: I'd sell off part of mine
To any Lombard usurer born and bred;
Cursed by this lack of cash, I wouldn't mind
The risk involved; let it be on my head.
No full purse hangs upon my belt: instead
It's this, Good God, that puts me at a loss,
That, without coins, I only come across
Crosses of wood or stone; but if my fate
Is to behold at last the one true cross,*
You will lose nothing but the time you wait.   30

Prince du lis, qui à tout bien complest,
Que pansés vous comment il me desplaist,
Quant je ne puis venir à mon entente.
Bien m'entendez, aydés moy, s'il vous plaist,
Vous n'y perdrés seulement que l'attente.

Au doiz de la letre :

Allés, letres, faictes ung sault,
Quoyque n'aiez piés ne langue,
Remonstrez en vostre harangue
Que faulte d'argent si m'assault.

Prince of the lily, friend to every good,
Think how it hurts when all that I've pursued
And what I long for proves so hard to get.
Help me, I beg, I know you've understood:
You will lose nothing but the time you wait.

On the back of the letter

Go to it, letter, at the double,
Although you've neither foot nor tongue,
And make it clear in your harangue
That lack of cash is all my trouble.

VII – *Epître à ses amis*

Aiez pictié, aiez pictié de moy,
A tout le moins, s'i vous plaist, mes amis !
En fosse giz, non pas soubz houz ne may,
En cest exil ouquel je suis transmis
Par Fortune, comme Dieu l'a permis.
Filles amans jeunes gens et nouveaulx,
Danceurs, saulteurs faisans les piez de veaux,
Vifz comme dars, aguz comme aguillon,
Gousiers tintans clers comme gascaveaux —
Le lesserez là, le povre Villon ?

Chantres chantans à plaisances, sans loy,
Galans rians, plaisans en faiz et diz,
Coureux alans, francs de faulx or, d'aloy,
Gens d'esperit, ung petit estourdiz,
Trop demourez, car il meurt entandiz.
Faiseurs de laiz, de motés et rondeaux,
Quant mort sera, vous lui ferez chaudeaux !
Où gist, il n'entre n'escler ne tourbillon ;
De murs espoix on lui a fait bandeaux —
Le lesserez là, le povre Villon ?

Venez le voir en ce piteux arroy,
Nobles hommes, francs de quars et de dix,
Qui ne tenez d'empereur ne de roy,
Mais seulement de Dieu de Paradiz,
Jeuner lui fault dimenches et merdiz,
Dont les dens a plus longues que ratteaux ;
Après pain sec (non pas après gasteaux)
En ses boyaulx verse eaue à groz boullon
Bas en terre — table n'a ne tresteaux —
Le lesserez là, le povre Villon ?

VII – *Letter to His Friends**

Have pity now, have pity upon me,
All those of you, at least, who are my friends!
For I'm not stretched beneath the hawthorn tree
But in a prison pit, where I've been sent
By Fortune who, no doubt, has God's consent.
Lasses that go for men who kick their heels
And prance like tumblers in the jig or reel,
As swift as darts, sharp goads to spur you on,
Your small throats chiming out a merry peal –
Will you leave him to lie there, poor Villon?   10

Singers who spurn the rules, all fancy-free,
And laughing lads who charm the girls no end,
With neither forged nor legal currency,
Bright witty chaps, a little scatterbrained,
He's dying while you fellows hang around.
Makers of lays, rondeaux, motets and all,
When he's already dead you'll send hot meals!
No whirlwind shakes the bed he lies upon,
He's safe from lightning, swaddled by thick walls –
Will you leave him to lie there, poor Villon?   20

A parlous state he lives in; come and see,
You untaxed, untithed nobles who depend
Upon no king or emperor but are free
To take whatever God in heaven sends.
Sundays and Tuesdays, both these days he spends
Fasting with rake-like teeth; after his meal
(Dry bread, not cake), he pours a monstrous deal
Of water in his belly, gulps it down,
Sprawled on the floor – no table and no stool –
Will you leave him to lie there, poor Villon?   30

Princes nommez, ancïens, jouvenciaulx,
Impetrez moy graces et royaulx seaulx
Et me montez en quelque corbillon.
Ainsi le font l'un à l'autre pourceaux,
Car où l'un brait, ilz fuyent à monceaux —
Le lesserez là, le povre Villon ?

Let all you princes, young and old, appeal
For my full pardon under royal seal,
Or hoist me in a basket you've sent down.
That is the way the very swine must feel:
They rush to help the pig who starts to squeal –
Will you leave him to lie there, poor Villon?

VIII – Débat de Villon et de son cœur

Qu'est ce que j'oy ? *Ce suis je.* Qui ? *Ton cueur,*
Qui ne tient mais qu'à ung petit filet :
Force n'ay plus, substance ne liqueur,
Quant je te voy retrait ainsi seulet
Com povre chien tapi en reculet.
Pour quoy est ce ? *Par ta folle plaisance.*
Que t'en chault il ? *J'en ay grant desplaisance.*
Laisse m'en paix ! *Pour quoy ?* G'y penseray.
Quant sera ce ? Quant seray hors d'enfance.
Plus ne t'en dit. Et je m'en passeray.

Que penses tu ? Estre homme de valeur.
Tu as trente ans ! C'est l'aage d'ung mulet.
Est ce enfance ? Nennil. *C'est donc foleur*
Qui te saisist. Par où ? Par le collet ?
Rien n'y congnois. Si faiz ! *Quoy ?* Mousche en lait :
L'ung est blanc, l'autre noire. C'est distance !
Est ce donc tout ? Que veux tu ? Que je tence ?
Se n'est assez, je recommenceray.
Tu es perdu ! G'y mectray resistence.
Plus ne t'en dis. Et je m'en passeray.

J'en ay le dueil ; toi le mal et douleur.
Se feusses ung povre ydiot et folet,
Encore eusses de t'excuser couleur ;
Si n'as tu soing, tout t'est ung, bel ou lait.
Ou la teste as plus dure q'un jalet,
Ou mieulx te plaist qu'onneur ceste meschance :
Que respondras à ceste consequence ?
J'en seray hors quant je trespasseray.
Dieux, quel confort ! Quelle sage eloquence !
Plus ne t'en dis. Et je m'en passeray.

VIII – Debate between Villon and His Heart*

What's this I hear? *It's me.* Who's that? *Your heart,*
Now hanging by a single little thread,
I've no more strength or substance, blood departs
When I see you alone, dispirited,
Like some stray skulking dog who hides his head.
Why's this? *Your life is pleasure-mad and vain.*
What's that to you? *I pay the price in pain.*
Leave me in peace. *Why so?* I'll think about it.
When will that be? The day my childhood's done.
I'll say no more. And I can do without it.   10

Who do you think you are? A worthy man.
You're thirty now. The lifespan of a mule.
You call that childhood? No. *It's madness then*
That's seized you. By the collar? *You're a fool*
Who doesn't know a thing. Wrong. I can tell
Flies from the milk, one's black and one is white.
That's all? You want a quarrel, am I right?
Still not enough? Just wait till I get started.
You're dead and done for! Not without a fight.
I'll say no more. And I can do without it.   20

I have the heartache of it, you the pain.
If you were some poor fool or idiot, there
Might still be some excuse that you could feign;
But you don't care, all's one, the foul or fair.
Either your head's a rock or you prefer
Such misery to honour and content:
What can you answer to this argument?
Once I am dead I won't think much about it.
There's comfort for you! Wise and eloquent!
I'll say no more. And I can do without it.   30

Dont vient ce mal ? Il vient de mon mal eur :
Quant Saturne me fist mon fardelet,
Ces motz y mist, je le croy. *C'est foleur :*
Son seigneur es, et te tiens son varlet !
Voy que Salmon escrit en son rolet :
« L'homme sage, ce dit il, a puissance
Sur les estoilles et sur leur influence. »
Je n'en croy riens : tel qu'ilz m'ont fait seray.
Que dis tu dea ? Certes, c'est ma creance.
Plus ne t'en dis. Et je m'en passeray.

Veux tu vivre ? Dieu m'en doint la puissance !
Il te fault… Quoy ? *Remors de consciënce,*
Lire sans fin. Et quoy lire ? *En science ;*
Laisser les folz. Bien j'y adviseray.
Or le retiens ! J'en ay bien souvenance.
N'attens pas trop, qu'il ne tiengne à plaisance !
Plus ne t'en dis. Et je m'en passeray.

These evils come from where? From my ill luck;
When Saturn bent to pack my little load,
He slipped in words of woe. *That's silly talk:*
You think that you're his servant, you're his lord!
Go read the scroll where Solomon wrote these words:
"The wise man has the power to defy
*The influence of all the stars on high".**
I'll be what they have made me, never doubt it.
What's that you say? My creed, I don't deny.
I'll say no more. And I can do without it.   40

So do you want to live? God grant me force!
In need… Of what? *I'd say sincere remorse,*
Long reading. Reading what? *God's natural laws;*
Leave fools. Well yes, I'll try and get it sorted.
Only remember. Yes, I will, of course.
No waiting for the perfect time and place!
I'll say no more. And I can do without it.

IX – Ballade contre les ennemis de la France

Rancontré soit des bestes feu gectans
Que Jason vit, querant la Thoison d'or,
Ou transmué d'omme en beste sept ans
Ainsi que fut Nabugodonosor,
Ou ait guerre et perte aussi villaine
Que Troies ot pour la prise d'Elayne,
Ou mis de fait soit avec Tantalus
Et Proserpine es infernaulx palus,
Ou plus que Job soit en griefve souffrance,
Tenant prison en la tour Dedalus,
Qui mal voudroit au royaume de France !

Quatre mois soit en ung vivier chantans,
La teste au fons, ainsi que le butor,
Ou au Grand Turcq vendu deniers contans
Pour estre mis au harnoys comme ung tor,
Ou trente ans soit, comme fut Magdelaine,
Sans drap vestir de linge ne de layne,
Ou soit noié comme fut Narcisus,
Ou aux cheveux comme Absalon pendus
Ou comme Judas fut par Desesperance,
Ou puist mourir comme Simon Magus,
Qui mal voudroit au royaume de France !

D'Octovïen puist revenir le temps,
C'est qu'on luy coulle ou ventre son tresor,
Ou qu'il soit mis entre meulles flotans
En ung moulin, comme fut sainct Victor,
Ou transglouty en la mer, sans alaine,
Pis que Jonas ou corps d'une ballaine,
Ou soit bany de la clarté Phebus,
Des biens Juno et des solas Venus,
Et du dieu Mars soit pugny à oultrance
Ainsi que fut roy Sardanapalus,
Qui mal voudroit au royaume de France !

IX – Ballade against the Enemies of France*

May he be met with beasts who breathe out flame,
Like Jason when he sought the Golden Fleece,
Or be like Nebuchadnezzar for the same
Long seven years transformed from man to beast;
Or fight and suffer a defeat as sore
As Troy's when Helen's rape provoked a war;
Or sent with Proserpine and Tantalus
To the infernal swamp as terminus;
Or suffer more than Job in his mischance,
Imprisoned in the tower of Daedalus –   10
Who wishes evil on the realm of France!

May he spend four months in a pond head down
To sing the way a heron does or croak,
Or get sold off to the Grand Turk, cash down,
And fitted with the ox's heavy yoke;
Or, like poor Magdalen, thirty years in full
Wear not a stitch of linen or of wool;
Or else be drowned as was Narcissus fair,
Or hanged perhaps like Absalom by his hair
Or by Despair like Judas from a branch,   20
Or crash like Simon Magus from the air –
Who wishes evil on the realm of France!

Oh for Octavian's age! So one could fill
His guts to busting with his molten gold,
Or lash him to the stones that work the mill
And grind him down, St Victor's fate of old;
Or, swallowed by the sea, where breath would fail,
May he fare worse than Jonah in the whale;
Or let him be exiled from Phoebus' light
Or Juno's wealth or Venus's delight,   30
Be punished by all pains that Mars invents
(Like King Sardanapalus, set alight) –
Who wishes evil on the realm of France!

Prince, porté soit des serfs Yolus
En la forest où domine Glocus
Et soit privé de paix et d'esperance ;
Car digne n'est de possider vertus
Qui mal voudroit au royaume de France !

Prince, let Aeolus' slaves bear him away
To sea-deep woods where Glaucus still holds sway,
Let him lose peace and hope of better chance;
Unworthy of all virtues he must be
Who wishes evil on the realm of France!

X – *Ballade de bon conseil*

Hommes failliz, despourveuz de raison,
Desnaturez et hors congnoissance,
Desmis du sens, comblez de desraison,
Folz abusez, plains de descongnoissance,
Qui procurez contre vostre naissance,
Vous submettans à detestable mort
Par lascheté, las ! Que ne vous remort
L'orribleté qui à honte vous maine ?
Voyez comment maint jeunes homs est mort
Par offensser et prendre autruy demaine.

Chascun en soy voye sa mesprison !
Ne nous vengons, prenons en pacïence :
Nous congnoissons que ce monde est prison
Aux vertueux franchis d'impacïence.
Battre, rouiller, pour ce n'est pas scïence,
Tollir, ravir, piller, meurtrir à tort :
De Dieu ne chault, trop de verté se tort
Qui en telz faiz sa jeunesse demaine,
Dont à la fin ses poins doloureux tort,
Par offenser et prendre autruy demaine.

Que vault piper, flater, rire en trayson
Quester, mentir, affermer sans fiance,
Farcer, tromper, artifier poison,
Vivre en peché, dormir en deffiance
De son prouchain sans avoir confience ?
Pour ce conclus : de bien faisons effort,
Reprenons cueur, ayons en Dieu confort.
Nous n'avons jour certain en la sepmaine ;
De noz maulx ont noz parens le ressort,
Par offencer et prendre autruy demaine.

X – Ballade of Good Counsel

Weak men, whose minds are empty of all reason,
Devoid of knowledge and of common sense,
Unnatural, in love with your unreason,
Ungrateful fools, puffed up with ignorance,
Who work against your birth's inheritance
And yield to hateful death that lies ahead,
Alas, do you not see that you are led
By evil to a shameful end? Look there,
How such a host of young men now are dead
For harming others and taking what's theirs.   10

Let each man see his fault within himself,
Not seek revenge, in patience bear offence:
We know this world is but a prison cell
For virtuous unrebellious men; and hence
Fighting and brawls and robbery make no sense,
Nor looting, mugging, murdering. The youth
Cares not for God and turns his back on truth
Who wastes his time involved in such affairs;
One day he'll sit and wring his hands in ruth
For harming others and taking what's theirs.   20

Where does it lead, to fawn and fake a laugh,
To beg and swindle, swear what isn't true,
Lie, cheat and con, cook up some poisonous draught,
To live in sin, and toss the whole night through,
Distrusting neighbours with no trust in you?
Thus I conclude, let's work towards the good,
Take heart and find in God the strength we need.
In the whole week no day is sure; our heirs
And kinsmen pay the price of our misdeeds,
For harming others and taking what's theirs.   30

197

Vivons en paix, exterminons discord ;
Ieunes et vieulx, soyons tous d'ung accord :
La loy le veult, l'appostre le ramaine
Licitement en l'espitre rommaine.
Ordre nous fault, estat ou aucun port.
Nottons ces poins, ne laissons le vray port
Par offensser et prendre autruy demaine.

Virtuous men, let's live without discord,
In peace, both young and old, of one accord –
Law sent by God, and so St Paul declares,*
Let's heed the truth his Roman Letter bears;
Order we need, degree, or some support.
Note down these points, let's not leave our true port
For harming others and taking what's theirs.

XI – Probleme, Ballade de fortune

Fortune fuz par clercs jadiz nommée,
Que toy, Françoys, crye et nomme murtriere,
Qui n'es homme d'aucune renommée.
Meilleur que toy faiz user en plastriere
Par povreté, et fouyr en carriere.
S'à honte viz, te dois tu doncques plaindre ?
Tu n'es pas seul, si ne te dois complaindre.
Regarde et voy, de mes faiz de jadiz,
Mains vaillans homs par moy mors et roiddiz,
Et n'es, ce sais, envers eulx ung soullon.
Appaise toy et mect fin en tes diz :
Par mon conseil prens tout en gré, Villon !

Contre grans roys me suis bien anymée
Le temps qui est passé ça en arriere.
Priame occis et toute son armée :
Ne lui valut tour, donjon ne barriere.
Et Hannibal, demoura il derriere ?
En Cartaige par mort le feiz actaindre,
Et Scypïon l'Affrequain feit estaindre.
Julius Cesar au Senat je vendiz.
En Egipte Pompée je perdiz.
En mer noyay Jazon en ung boullon,
Et une foys Romme et Rommains ardiz.
Par mon conseil prens tout en gré, Villon !

Alixandre, qui tant fist de hemée
Qu'il voulut voir l'estoille poucyniere,
Sa personne par moy fut envelimée.
Alphasar roy, en champ, sur sa baniere
Ruay jus mort. Cela est ma maniere :
Ainsi l'ay fait, ainsi le maintendray,
Autre cause ne raison n'en rendray.
Holofernés l'idolastre mauldiz,

XI – Problem, Ballade of Fortune*

Fortune they named me, scholars long ago,
And now, François, you call me murderess –
Yes, you, without a touch of fame to show.
I've sent your betters, poor men in distress,
To sweat in lime-kilns or break stone for less.
You whinge and moan because you live in shame?
You're not the only one, so don't complain.
Look round and see the feats I did of old,
The valiant men I laid out stiff and cold,
Compared to them you're just a scullion.   10
Calm down, I say, shut up for once, don't scold:
Take my advice and take what comes, Villon!

Against the greatest kings I fought to show
My power in ancient times, in days long past.
Priam I killed and all his army too,
No tower or bulwark kept him safe at last.
Could Hannibal survive? At my behest
Death snuffed him out in Carthage, and the same
Fate befell African Scipio's bright flame.
And Caesar on the Senate floor I sold;   20
In Egypt I destroyed Pompey the Bold;
Jason was drowned – that whirlwind I brought on.
Once even Rome I burned: now you've been told –
Take my advice and take what comes, Villon!

Great Alexander shed much blood, and so
Wanted the Pleiades next on his list;
A little of my poison laid him low.
King Alphasar fought, but, when I struck his crest,
Fell on his flag. That's how I like it best:
That's what I do, I'll always do the same,   30
I don't see any reason to explain.
When I cursed Holofernes, he was killed

Qu'occist Judic — et dormoit entandiz —
De son poignart dedens son pavillon.
Absallon, quoy ? En fuyant le pendis.
Par mon conseil prens tout en gré, Villon.

Pour ce, Françoys, escoute que te dis :
Se riens peusse sans Dieu de Paradiz
A toy n'à autre ne demourroit haillon,
Car pour ung mal lors j'en feroye dix.
Par mon conseil prens tout en gré, Villon !

By Judith as he slept, a heathen felled
With his own sword in his pavilion;
Absalom? Hanged as he escaped the field.
Take my advice and take what comes Villon!

And so, François, listen to what you're told:
But for the fact that God in heaven holds
Me back, you wouldn't have a rag to put on:
I'd do ten wrongs for every one of old.   40
Take my advice and take what comes, Villon!

XII – *Ballade des pendus*

Freres humains, qui après nous vivez,
N'ayez les cueurs contre nous endurcis,
Car, se pitié de nous povres avez,
Dieu en aura plus tost de vous mercis.
Vous nous voiez cy attachez, cinq, six :
Quant de la chair, que trop avons nourrie,
El est pieça devorée et pourrie,
Et nous, les os, devenons cendre et pouldre.
De nostre mal personne ne se rie,
Mais priez Dieu que tous nous vueille absouldre.

Se freres vous clamons, pas n'en devez
Avoir desdaing, quoy que fusmes occis
Par justice… touteffois vous sçavez
Que tous hommes n'ont pas le sens rassis.
Excusez nous, puis que sommes transis,
Envers le filz de la Vierge Marie,
Que sa grace ne soit pour nous tarie,
Nous preservant de l'infernale fouldre.
Nous sommes mors, ame ne nous harie
Mais priez Dieu que tous nous vueille absouldre.

La pluye nous a debuez et lavez
Et le soleil deseichez et noircis.
Pies, corbeaulx nous ont les yeulx cavez
Et arraché la barbe et les sourcilz.
Jamais nul temps nous ne sommes assis :
Puis ça, puis là, comme le vent varie,
A son plaisir sans cesse nous charie,
Plus becquetez d'oyseaulx que dez à coudre.
Ne soiez donc de nostre confrairie,
Mais priez Dieu que tous nous vueille absouldre.

XII – Ballade of the Hanged Men*

Men, human brothers, who live after us,
Let not your hearts be hardened, for if you
Can feel some pity for our wretchedness,
The sooner you'll receive God's mercy too.
You see five, six of us, strung up to view:
As for the flesh that once we overfed,
Here's where it rots, itself devoured instead,
And we, the bones, to dust and ashes fall.
Let no one mock our misery or deride,
But pray to God that He forgive us all.   10

If brothers we have called you, do not go
Away indignant, for there's no offence.
Yes, we were slain by Justice… but you know
That not all men are born with your good sense.
We have no voice, being stiff and cold long since,
So intercede for us with Mary's Son
That His clear fount of grace may ever run
And thus preserve us from the flames of Hell.
Let no one come to trouble us, dead men,
But pray to God that He forgive us all.   20

The rain has washed us clean and soaked us through,
The sun has dried us up, blackened and seared;
Our eyes gouged out by crows and magpies who
Have plucked away our eyebrows and our beards.
Never one moment are we still, but stirred
And dangled to and fro by every wind,
The birds have pecked at us until our skin
Is like a housewife's thimble, pocked with holes.
Don't join the confraternity we're in,
But pray to God that He forgive us all.   30

Prince Jesus, qui sur tous a maistrie
Garde qu'Enfer n'ait de nous seigneurie :
A luy n'ayons que faire ne que souldre.
Humains, icy n'a point de mocquerie,
Mais priez Dieu que tous nous vueille absouldre.

Prince Jesus, lord of everything that is,
Preserve us from the power of the abyss:
We've no accounts to settle down in hell.
Men, there's no cause for mockery in this,
But pray to God that He forgive us all,

XIII – Quatrain

Je suis François, dont il me poise,
Né de Paris emprès Pontoise,
Et de la corde d'une toise
Saura mon col que mon cul poise.

XIII – Quatrain*

I am François, hard name to bear,
Born Paris, though Pontoise is near,
And from a six-foot rope it's here
My neck shall learn the weight of my rear.

XIV – *Louange et requête à la Cour*

Tous mes cinq sens, yeulx, oreilles et bouche,
Le nez et vous, le sensitif, aussi,
Tous mes membres, ou il y a reprouche,
En son endroit ung chascun die ainsi :
« Souveraine Court, par qui sommes icy,
Vous nous avez gardez de desconfire !
Or la langue seule ne peut suffire
A vous rendre suffisantes louenges ;
Si parlons tous, fille du souverain Sire,
Mere des bons et seur des benoistz anges. »

Cueur, fendés vous, ou percez d'une broche,
Et ne soiez au moins plus endurcy
Qu'au desert fut la forte bise roche
Dont le peuple des Juifz fut adoulcy.
Fondez lermes et venez à mercy,
Com humble cueur qui tendrement souspire ;
Louez la Court conjointe au saint empire,
L'heur des François, le confort des estranges,
Procréée lassus au ciel empire,
Mere des bons et seur des benoistz anges.

Et vous, mes dens, chascune si s'esloche,
Saillez avant, rendez toutes mercy
Plus haultement qu'oncques trompe ne cloche,
Et de mascher n'ayés ores soussi.
Considerez que je fusse transi,
Foye, polmon, et rate qui respire ;
Et vous, mon corps — ou vil estes et pire
Qu'ours ne pourcel qui fait son nic es fanges —
Louez la Court, devant qu'il vous empire,
Mere des bons et seur des benoistz anges.

XIV – *Praise and Request of the Court**

All my five senses, ears and mouth and eyes
Nose too, and you, the sense of touch, of course,
And every part (lest some reproach arise)
Plead on its own behalf, and speak out thus:
"Sovereign Court, you are the only cause
Why we're still here, not down among the dead.
Language alone is not enough to laud
And praise you for the justice you have done;
So speak we all, child of the Sovereign Lord,
Sister of angels, mother of good men."   10

Heart, break in two, be pierced upon a spit,
Or be no harder, at the very least,
Than was the desert's great dark rock* that split
To quench the Jews' fierce anger and their thirst:
Weep, weep, in all humility and burst
With tears of sorrow and a tender sigh;
Extol the Court, one with that realm on high,
The joy of France, the foreigner's defence
Engendered in the empyreal sky,
Sister of angels, mother of good men.   20

And you, my teeth, jump to it, come and tell
What thanks you offer with no more ado,
More loudly than a trumpet or a bell;
No need to worry whether you can chew.
Just think, I could be stiff and cold by now:
You liver, spleen and lungs who breathe the air,
And body (or you're vile and worse by far
Than any pig slouched in its dungy den)
All praise the Court lest foul should follow fair,
Sister of angels, mother of good men.   30

Prince, trois jours ne vueillez m'escondire
Por moy pourvoir et aux miens adieu dire :
Sans eulx argent je n'ay, icy n'aulx changes.
Court triumphant, *fiat*, sans me desdire,
Mere des bons et seur des benoistz anges !

Prince, grant me three more days to see things through,
Get ready, and then bid my friends adieu:
Without them I'm flat broke, the banks won't lend.
Say *fiat*, Court, and don't refuse me now,
Sister of angels, mother of good men.

XV – Question au clerc du guichet

Que dictes vous de mon appel,
Garnier ? Fis je sens ou folie ?
Toute beste garde sa pel :
Qui la contraint, efforce ou lie,
S'elle peut, elle se deslie.
Quant dont, par plaisir voluntaire,
Chanté me fut ceste omelie,
Estoit il lors temps de moy taire ?

Se fusse des hoirs Hue Capel,
Qui fut extrait de boucherie,
On ne m'eust parmy ce drapel
Fait boire en ceste escorcherie —
— Vous entendez bien joncherie —.
Mais quant ceste paine arbitraire
On me juga par tricherie,
Estoit il lors temps de moy taire ?

Cuydiés vous que soubz mon capel
N'eust autant de philosophie
Comme de dire : « J'en appel » ?
Si avoit, je vous certifie.
— Combien que point trop ne m'y fie —.
Quant dit me me fut, present notaire,
« Pendu serés », je vous affie,
Estoit il lors temps de moy taire ?

Prince, se j'eusse eu la pepie,
Pieçà je fusse où est Clotaire :
Aux champs, debout comme une espie.
Estoit il lors temps de moy taire ?

XV – Question to the Prison Clerk*

Garnier, tell me what you think:
Did this appeal make sense or not?
A beast looks after his own skin,
Beaten or trapped or tied, he'll get
Free if he can and slip the knot.
So when, out of the blue, they sang
Me such a homily on the spot,
Was that a time to hold my tongue?

If I'd been heir to Hugh Capet*
(Born of a butcher's line, I think),   10
They would have found some other way
Than using cloth to make me drink*
– With you I need not be more frank.
But when, beneath that penalty,
Wrongly imposed, I almost sank,
Was that a time to hold my tongue?

You think my cap does not conceal
Enough philosophy to force
Out two short words like "I appeal"?
I certify it does, of course,   20
Though I'm not sure things can't get worse.
When I was told "You are to hang"
(With notary present to endorse),
Was that a time to hold my tongue?

Prince, if I'd lost my voice, I'd be
As dead as old Clotaire,* and hung
To keep stiff watch in fields: now say,
Was that a time to hold my tongue?

Note on the Text

The French text given here is based on that of Jean Rychner and Albert Henry (Geneva, 1974–85), which has now superseded Longnon and Foulet (1932) as the standard scholarly edition.

I have also profited from the more recent editions of Claude Thiry (Paris, 1991) and Barbara Sargent-Baur (Toronto, 1994). My choice among variant readings has sometimes been governed by what seemed most amenable to translation. For the convenience of readers I have maintained the familiar titles derived from editorial tradition ("Of the Ladies of Past Time", "Of the Hanged Men", etc.). Italics are used to indicate house signs, often of taverns and brothels.

A real understanding of Villon requires far more background information than can be contained within the usual limits of annotation. I have, therefore, followed the example of some recent editors in supplementing the Notes with an Index of the many unfamiliar names and places mentioned in the poetry, while omitting the more obvious classical and biblical references. Ideally, the Notes should be sufficient for a first reading, while the Index should satisfy the kind of curiosity that Villon usually provokes.

Like most popular editions of Villon, this volume excludes the eleven *Ballades en jargon*, written in the near-incomprehensible slang of thieves.

Notes

THE LEGACY

16, *broken heart*: In a parody of courtly love poetry, Villon presents his decision to leave Paris for Angers as the result of an unhappy love affair: he was, in fact, attempting to escape the consequences of his participation in the robbery at the Collège de Navarre.

72, *also my pavilion*: Villon amuses himself by assuming the appurtenances of a great lord; the pavilion is as illusory as the fame that he leaves to his adoptive father. The same applies to many other bequests: the coat of mail, the dogs, etc. An essential aspect of Villon's satirical strategy is to offer gifts that initially sound impressive, but turn out to be non-existent or worthless.

90, *The White Horse and The Mule*: Hinting at the impotence of Saint-Amant and the sterility of his wife (see T 1006–13). Throughout *The Legacy* and the *Testament* Villon plays with the signs that, in the Paris of his day, served to identify houses, shops and taverns. Stealing or displacing these signs was a common student prank.

95, *Carmelite Bull*: A papal bull of 1409 gave the Mendicant orders, including the Carmelites, the right to hear confessions. Against this decision the secular clergy cited a decretal of the Lateran Council (1215), which stated that all the faithful of both sexes (*omnis utriusque sexus*) should confess at least once a year to the parish priest.

138, *Nijon's stony heap*: Almost all the castles named in the *Legacy* and the *Testament* are in a ruinous state after the Hundred Years' War (1337–1453).

145, *a knight*: Jean de Harlay, commander of the Night Watch, whose claim to knighthood was much disputed (see T 1828).

151, *Three Lily Buds*: One of the prisons at the Châtelet, which here makes its first menacing appearance in Villon's poetry. The ironic suggestion is that he would be as comfortable at the Châtelet as at an inn. There is an untranslatable pun on *lys* (lily) and *lit* (bed): prisoners slept on the floor.

160, *plough his field*: Erotic injunction; *The Pine Cone* was obviously equipped to serve a variety of appetites.

163, *that lord*: Robert d'Estouteville, Provost of Paris.

166, *slipper soles*: Fit only for summer wear.

177, *Perrenet Marchant*: Officer at the Châtelet, perhaps Villon's rival in love; a favourite target (see T 764, 937, 1094–95).

195, *Loup... Cholet*: Corrupt policemen at the Châtelet.

196, *poor orphans*: Villon's antiphrastic term for the three rich usurers named in the following stanza (see T 1275).

208, *when I am old*: When Villon is old the three usurers will be not where they eat but where they are eaten.

209, *nomination*: Official university document certifying a graduate's right to apply for an ecclesiastical benefice.

219, *humble clerks*: Antiphrasis: Cotin and de Vitry were wealthy canons of Notre-Dame (see T 1306)

225, *add a cross*: Complicated and untranslatable punning involving a bishop's pastoral rod, an inn sign and something like a billiard cue.

254, *Final Fifteen Signs*: Announcing the Last Judgement.

262, *vile assaults on me*: The unnamed author of these "vile assaults" may be Guy Tabarie, whose confession to the robbery at the Collège de Navarre implicated Villon.

263, *St Anthony's Fire*: Erysipelas, acute inflammation of the skin.

281, *trance*: For Villon's trance and the mockery of scholastic jargon see Extra Material, p. 234.

THE TESTAMENT

6, *Thibaud d'Aussigny*: The name of the hated Bishop of Orléans interrupts the sentence and sets off a long digression which postpones the dictation of the will. The bishop would have blessed the crowds in the streets of Orléans during the annual procession to celebrate Joan of Arc's delivery of the besieged city in 1429. As a clerk from the diocese of Paris, Villon denies that Thibaud d'Aussigny has any legal authority over him.

12, *his little deer*: A hint at the bishop's presumed homosexual tendencies.

37, *as Picards do*: A heretical prayer, assumed to be improvised and spontaneous rather than fixed and liturgical.

48, *Deus laudem*: Psalm 108 in the Vulgate; verse 7 reads: "Let his days be few and another take his office."

56, *King of France*: Louis XI, whose amnesty had freed Villon from the prison at Meung. Also referred to as "our late Dauphin", since his accession to the throne was relatively recent.

101, *goodly city*: The Emmaus of Villon's pilgrimage may have been Moulins, capital of the Dukes of Bourbon whose motto was *Espérance*.

210, *Sage*: Solomon as presumed author of the Book of Ecclesiastes from which both citations are literally translated (Ecclesiastes 11:9–10).

221: See Job 7:6.

264, *I have written*: Pilate's reply to the Jews (John 19:22)

292, *know of him no more*: Psalm 103:16.

329, *Ballade of the Ladies of Times Past*: See Index for the figures listed in this and the following ballade. The Prince addressed in the *envoi* is a conventional feature of the ballade form and need not indicate any specific individual.

454, *Fair Armouress*: Historical figure, once mistress of a rich canon of Notre-Dame, she was later reduced to poverty; her name appears in cathedral records.

533, *Glover Girl*: Like the Fair Armouress, all the girls listed in this ballade have fictitious employments adopted to avoid prosecution for prostitution.

565, *Dumb Fremin*: Villon's fictitious clerk.

625, *Double Ballade on the Same Topic*: See Index for figures listed in this ballade.

658, *beaten flat*: The episode is obscure, but involves some kind of brawl over a woman (Katherine de Vausselles) where both Villon and Noël Jolis got a good thrashing.

668, *one who loves a broomstick ride*: A sorcerer, and hence liable to be burned at the stake.

737, *Tacque the gay Thibaud*: Villon deliberately confuses the name of Bishop Thibaud d'Aussigny with that of Tacque Thibaud, the notorious homosexual minion of Duke Jean de Berry.

740, *chokepears*: An instrument of torture designed to stretch the jaws.

742, *et reliqua*: And all the rest.

752, *Lombard loves his God*: Lombard bankers were regarded as particularly rapacious.

757, *Testament*: Villon's *Legacy* was sometimes known as the *Little Testament*.

765, *bales of straw*: See L 177–84.

781, *no previous legatee*: The *Testament* does not exclude those who have already received bequests in *The Legacy*.

805, *prophets and patriarchs*: Villon reflects the orthodox view that, until Christ freed them through the Harrowing of Hell, the souls of the just who had died before the Incarnation resided in Limbo, where there was no suffering.

838, *Nine Orders*: The nine angelic orders.

858, *Devil's Fart*: A large phallic-shaped stone outside the house of Mme de Bruyères: attempts by students to move it elsewhere provoked frequent clashes with the police. The *Story of the Devil's Fart*, if it ever existed, would have made a rather inappropriate bequest to Guillaume Villon.

885–86, *Egyptian... Theophilus*: St Mary of Egypt, a converted courtesan who led an ascetic life in the desert; Theophilus made a pact with the Devil, but was saved by the intervention of the Virgin Mary.

942, *Ballade to his Ladylove*: The first two stanzas have the names of François and Marthe in acrostic. Marthe may be the rival or successor of Kate de Vausselles.

971, *sword I gave away*: See L 81–82.

978, *Lay*: In fact, a rondeau.

1013, *Mule... Red Ass*: Modifying the bequest made at L 89–96.

1025, *sword... sheath*: Villon's habitual sexual innuendo.

1050, *falconry*: Villon implies that, despite their aristocratic pretensions, the two rich drapers, Merebeuf and Louviers (see L 265–68), are incapable of such a noble sport.

1060, *Poitou*: To "speak Poitevin" was figuratively to speak in an ambiguous or deceptive way; Villon also takes the phrase literally and imitates the Poitou dialect in the next stanza.

1090, *lanyard*: A decoration for the uniform of the Paris police force (Eleven-Score Guard), but also a suggestion that they deserve to be hanged.

1097, *bar sinister*: Heraldic device indicating bastardy.

1102, *Cholet*: Ex-cooper, corrupt policeman, condemned for raising a false alarm in Paris. For Cholet and Loup see L 185–92.

1118, *Woodsmith*: nickname of Jean Mahé, torturer at the Châtelet.

1157, *abbess*: Huguette de Hamel, abbess of Port-Royal (Pourras), who embezzled the convent's money and absconded with her lover.

1195, *Green Cage*: Sign of the house where Friar Baude seeks to protect his whore (or his brothel) from harassment by the police.

1197, *Vauvert*: Ruined abbey near Paris, supposedly haunted by the Devil.

1272, *half a crown*: I have used pre-decimal British currency to suggest Marle's exorbitant exchange rates.

1275, *three poor orphans*: By antiphrasis, the three old usurers (L 201–2).

1287, *Ave salus, tibi decus*: Parody of Latin hymn to the Virgin with a pun on *tibi decus*: the Virgin gets honour (*decus*), the usurers get money (*d'écus*). The religion-money wordplay continues in the next stanza with *le grant Credo* – the Apostles' Creed and long-term credit, both equally alien to the three usurers.

1307, *under-clerks*: The two canons of Notre-Dame to whom Villon ceded his university "nomination" (L 217–18)

1347, *I left Bicêtre*: See bequest at L 140.

1378, *Ballade for Robert d'Estouteville*: The speaker is Robert d'Estouteville himself, the "Lord who still serves St Christopher"; the name of his wife, Ambroise de Loré, is given in acrostic in the first two stanzas.

1422, *Ballade of Malicious Tongues*: It is not known what provoked this unpleasantly excremental ballade.

1458, *Franc Gontier*: Idealized countryman in a poem by Philippe de Vitry. In another poem Pierre d'Ailly contrasted the simple life of Gontier with that of a rich tyrant (1459). The Sage (1461) is again Solomon: "Strive not with a mighty man, lest thou fall into his hands" (Ecclesiasticus 8:1).

1531, *Irish colleens*: Not to be found in Villon, but geographical precision is hardly essential to the poem and the *blarney-barney* rhyme is irresistible.

1555, *indulgence*: Villon's word is *pardon*, but the reference is clearly to the Catholic practice of "Indulgences" by which, in return for various pious acts, a Christian could obtain remittance of time he would otherwise have to spend in Purgatory. This could easily be understood as permission to commit sin for the period indicated.

1598, *bene stat*: "It is well" – an ironically courtly Latin statement.

1636, *Jolis*: Not his first thrashing (T 662).

1672, *Dicemont or Robbeville*: *Montpipeau* and *Rüel* suggest gambling and robbery. I have invented two French-sounding names that have the same effect in English.

1675, *Colin de Cayeux*: Villon's accomplice in the robbery at the Collège de Navarre, hanged in 1460.

1696, *body fries*: Forgers were plunged in boiling oil before being hanged.

1704, *farce and interlude*: Genres of the medieval popular theatre; it has been suggested that Villon joined a troupe of travelling players during his absence from Paris (1457–61).

1728, *Fifteen Twenties*: A hospice for the blind who were licensed to beg.

1734, *Innocents*: The largest Parisian cemetery.

1806, *Chartier*: Alain Chartier, author of the poem *La Belle Dame sans mercy*.

1820, *Seneschal*: Pierre de Brézé, a distinguished soldier who had fallen out of favour. Villon plays with the double sense of *maréchal* – as a high military rank and as *maréchal ferrant*, a blacksmith.

1828, *Captain of the Watch*: The pretentious Jean de Harlay (L 145)

1838, *dry mass*: An abbreviated form of the mass, without consecration or communion.

1869, *Sainte-Avoie*: Originally home to a community of pious widows, but by Villon's time a hostel for women with a less reputable past. The chapel was on the upper floor, so Villon could not have been interred there.

1896, *shaved him close*: When Villon was deprived of his clerical status by Bishop Thibaud d'Aussigny, his head would have been cropped close to cancel all sign of the tonsure.

1941, *Philippe Brunel*: The totally reprehensible Lord of Grigny, already on Villon's blacklist (L 137, T 1346).

1959, *Perrette's Hole*: Court for early form of tennis (*jeu de paume*); the wordplay is obvious.

MISCELLANEOUS POEMS

I – Ballade of the Proverbs: I, II and III are all conventional exercises in proverbial wisdom and anaphora.

II, 22, *Hussite heresy*: Heretical movement in Bohemia; its leader, Jan Hus, was condemned by the Council of Constance and burned at the stake in 1415.

III, 9, *in baths*: Bathhouses were known as sites for illicit amorous encounters.

IV– Ballade from the Contest at Blois: One of ten poems by different authors all beginning with the phrase "I die of thirst here where the fountain flows", taken from a poem by Charles d'Orléans: probably a collective compliment rather than a contest.

V, *In Praise of Marie d'Orléans... demittitur alto*: Marie d'Orléans was the daughter of Charles d'Orléans and Marie de Clèves; her birth in 1457 was an occasion for particular celebration in that the Duke's two previous marriages had produced no heir. The Latin epigraph is a citation from Virgil's messianic Eclogue IV: "Now a new generation descends from heaven on high". The first two stanzas refer to the Virgin Mary rather than to Marie d'Orléans, but the poem constantly blurs the distinction.

V, 21: *old Clovis's right side*: First Christian king of the Franks. The mention of "Caesar" six lines later is simply another affirmation of royal parentage.

V, 42–43, *Delectasti... factura tua*: "For thou, O Lord, hast made me glad through thy work". (Psalm 92:4).

V, 51–52, *Inimicum... laudabit*: "Consider as an enemy whoever praises you in your presence"; source unknown.

V, 108, *Patrem... proles*: "The child takes after the father", a proverb that hardly needs Villon's dubious attribution to Cato.

VI – Request to the Prince: An old subtitle identifies the Prince as "Monseigneur de Bourbon", but it is more likely to have been addressed to Charles d'Orléans.

VI, 18, *Pactay*: There were no woods around Pactay and, in any case, there was not much profit to be made out of chestnuts.

VI, 29, *the one true cross*: For Villon the cross stamped on coins rather than the Cross of Christ

VII – Letter to His Friends: Purports to be have been written during Villon's imprisonment at Meung in 1461. The friends to whom he appeals would seem to be itinerant entertainers and poets, antiphrastically addressed as "nobles" (22) because they share the aristocratic privilege of exemption from taxes.

VIII – Debate between Villon and His Heart: An allegorical debate poem. The distribution of the dialogue is not always clear.

VIII, 36–37: If Villon attributes these lines to Solomon, it is probably because they sound suitably sententious. The whole question of planetary influence was controversial, since the idea seemed to conflict with orthodox Catholic teaching on the freedom of the will.

IX – Ballade against the Enemies of France: See Index for names in this ballade. The authenticity of the poem has been challenged, but its patriotic verve recalls Villon's praise of Louis XI (T 56–72). The opening lines may point to the creation of the Order of the Golden Fleece by Philip the Good, Duke of Burgundy. Philip's own dynastic ambitions conflicted with those of Louis XI, making him, therefore, one of the "enemies of France".

X, 33, *so St Paul declares*: "Be of the same mind one towards another... live peaceably with all men" (Romans 12, 16–18).

XI – Problem, Ballade of Fortune: See Index for the figures listed in this ballade.

XII – Ballade of the Hanged Men: Modern scholars have cast doubt on the old assumption that this poem was written after Villon's condemnation. The subject is plural and Villon, in any case, did not need to wait for 1462 to contemplate the likely end of his career.

XIII – Quatrain: Short enough to have been written in the days after Villon had been condemned to death in 1461. The definition of Paris as being near Pontoise is an old joke.

XIV – Praise and Request of the Court: Praise addressed to the Parlement of Paris, the highest secular court, which had commuted Villon's sentence from hanging to exile. The request is for a short delay so that he can put his affairs in order.

XIV, 13, *great dark rock*: The rock in Horeb from which Moses brought forth water (Exodus 17:1–6).

XV – Question to the Prison Clerk: This celebration of Villon's successful appeal in 1463 is addressed to Étienne Garnier, clerk or doorkeeper of the Châtelet prison.

XV, 9, *Hugh Capet*: Tenth-century King of the Francs, founder of Capetian dynasty.

XV, 12, *using cloth to make me drink*: A form of torture where water is forced into the victim's mouth through a cloth.

XV, 26, *Clotaire*: Sixth-century King of the Franks. The expression sounds proverbial: to be with Clotaire is to be long dead.

Extra Material

on

François Villon's

*The Testament
and Other Poems*

François Villon's Life

The poetry of François Villon accords a quite extraordinary prominence to the poet's own name. It is announced in the opening stanza of *The Legacy* ("I, a scholar, François Villon"), it is repeated in the 'Epitaph' of *The Testament*, it signs off the poem for Marie d'Orléans, it serves as a refrain for the 'Letter to His Friends' and for the 'Ballade of Fortune', it keeps turning up as an acrostic. There is something disturbing about this need to assert authorial identity, something that suggests an underlying anxiety; and indeed when we turn from the poetry to the historical record we find that the very name is problematic. As a university student up to 1452, Villon is François de Montcorbier; in 1456, as the accused in a murder case, he is first "François de Monterbier" and then "François des Loges, otherwise known as Villon"; he will be François Villon for the rest of his troubled career. What we know of that career comes to us from three sources: the archives of the University of Paris, legal documentation relating to his involvement in three serious crimes, and finally, of course, his own poetry, with its deceptively confessional stance. The outline they provide has gaps that make speculation irresistible.

Villon was born in Paris, probably in 1431. Despite what to modern readers is the rather high-sounding family name of "de Montcorbier", his parents were, the poet tells us, poor folk with no pretensions to nobility (T 273–80). While still a child, probably after the death of his father, he was adopted by Guillaume de Villon, professor of canon law and chaplain at Saint-Benoît-le-Bétourné near the Sorbonne. Guillaume proved to be a "more than father" and gave the boy a good religious and classical education, leading to the University of Paris, where he completed first the baccalaureate and then, in 1452, the licentiate and master's degree. These were the basic studies that qualified him as a "clerk", enjoying the privileges of clerical status.

Birth and Studies

He would now have been expected to proceed to higher studies in the faculties of law or theology; but Villon, by his own admission, was not of a scholarly disposition and was soon drawn to the less reputable side of Parisian student life (T 201–8). In June 1455 he was charged with murder after a brawl that ended with the fatal stabbing of a priest called Philippe Sermoise. Under the false name of "Michel Mouton", Villon had his own wounds

First Troubles with the Law

tended by a barber-surgeon, and then fled Paris in order to avoid arrest. In January 1456, however, he was able to return to the capital after receiving letters of pardon that accepted his plea of self-defence, noted his previous irreproachable conduct and recalled the forgiveness accorded by Sermoise on his deathbed.

Robbery at the Collège de Navarre

No such excuses could mitigate Villon's next crime. At Christmas 1456 he took part in what seems to have been a well-planned break-in at the Collège de Navarre. That this was indeed a professional job is suggested both by the amount of the haul (500 gold *écus*) and by the backgrounds of his partners, who included Petit-Jean, a noted cracksman, and Colin de Cayeux, later hanged as a member of the infamous Coquillard gang. At first luck seemed to be on Villon's side, for the robbery was not discovered until March 1457, by which time he had decamped to Angers, probably hoping to profit from his literary talents at the court of René d'Anjou. There was, in any case, nothing to connect him with the case until, in May of the same year, one of his accomplices, the garrulous clerk Guy Tabarie, chose to boast of his exploits to a drinking companion, who turned out to be an informer. Tabarie was arrested, tortured and finally released on payment of fifty *écus* after a full confession that implicated Villon.

Years on the Run

The poet's movements during the following five years are not known in any detail: he was beyond the reach of Parisian justice, but apparently unable to find any lasting place of refuge. Two episodes, however, stand out clearly. The first is a stay at the court of Charles d'Orléans at Blois in 1457–58. Charles d'Orléans was both a patron of poets and a distinguished poet himself; but if Villon hoped to be offered some kind of official position, he was disappointed. Though there are some signs that he tried briefly to write in an appropriately courtly manner, anything like a real meeting of minds was unlikely and the Duke's followers seem to have been hostile to the Parisian interloper.

Arrest and Release

The second and more significant episode is Villon's imprisonment by the Bishop of Orléans, Thibaud d'Aussigny, at Meung-sur-Loire during the summer of 1461. What he had done between 1458 and 1461 to deserve such punishment we do not know, though there is some indication that he may have disgraced himself by joining a company of itinerant entertainers (P VII). It must, in any case, have been something that, in the bishop's eyes, disqualified him as a clerk, for, among the many privations and tortures listed in the *Testament,* he recalls the brutal erasing of the tonsure that was the sign of clerical status (T 1896–97). Thus degraded, Villon had, at least, the good fortune to be released in October 1461, when Louis XI on his royal progress through Meung granted the amnesty customary on such occasions.

Once again one can only speculate as to why Villon took the risk of returning to Paris in 1462. Perhaps he was simply at the end of his tether, perhaps he hoped that he would receive the same lenient treatment as Guy Tabarie. And indeed, when his presence in the city became known to the Collège de Navarre, he fared rather better than he deserved. The college, it seems, was more interested in recuperating its losses than in exacting exemplary justice, and on 7th November, after admitting his guilt, Villon was released on condition that he repay his share of the loot – 120 gold *écus* – over a period of three years.

Return to Paris

It is hard to see how the college could have expected an unemployed ex-clerk to find such a sum; perhaps they had received some assurances from Guillaume de Villon. As things turned out, it took three weeks rather than three years for Villon to dash any hopes that he might be ready to mend his ways.

At the end of that same month he was caught up in an affray that concluded with the wounding of the pontifical notary Ferrebouc, who had participated in the interrogation of Villon's old accomplice Guy Tabarie. In Villon's defence, it must be said that he did not strike the blow and that the wound did not prove fatal. But the authorities had had enough. Arrested, imprisoned and tortured at the Châtelet, Villon was condemned to be "strangled and hanged". This, however, was not quite the end of the story, and the poet was not to die the death that his verses had sometimes seemed to predict. He appealed to the court of Parlement and, on 5th January 1463, the sentence was commuted to one of ten years' banishment from Paris. After being granted three days to put his affairs in order, Villon left the city, and that is the last we hear of him. Given his incorrigible character and the physical sufferings already endured, he is unlikely to have survived for long. The poems continued to circulate in manuscript and were first printed in 1489; but by the time of Clément Marot's edition of 1533, Villon was already becoming a figure of folklore as a witty rogue, professional prankster and hard-drinking con man. His reputation as a poet was not to recover until the nineteenth century, when French romanticism rediscovered him as the archetypal outsider.

New Arrest, Death Sentence, Pardon and Exile

François Villon's Audience

Seventy years after the reprieved poet took his last leave of Paris, the best of his early editors, Clément Marot, complained that to understand Villon fully "one would need to have lived in the Paris of his time and to have known the places, things and men that he speaks of: the more these things pass out of memory, the less men will understand the value of his legacies". The industry of modern scholarship has defied Marot's pessimistic forecast by identifying almost every character in the *Legacy* and the *Testament*; and yet the reader still has to come to terms with the difficulty of a poetry that often seems addressed only to a highly restricted and complicit audience with sufficient inside knowledge to decipher Villon's multiple ambiguities and autobiographical allusions. This exclusively Parisian audience would be familiar with the various and sometimes overlapping groups who provide the cast (not necessarily the readership) of the *Testament* – the lawyers and officials at the Châtelet with its law courts and prisons that Villon was to know only too well, the powerful financiers and usurers, the newly rich merchant class, the small tradesmen and artisans, the churchmen (both secular clergy and preaching orders), the underworld of whores, pimps and thieves. At the same time, Villon's readers would need to share enough of his own learning to respond appropriately to the sophisticated use of biblical, classical and French literary sources. Everything, therefore, points to an audience largely composed of clerks and including a core of initiates personally acquainted with the poet himself – the "lost boys" to whom Villon addresses two ballades towards the end of the *Testament* (T 1668–1719).

The term "clerk" was normally reserved for those who had completed basic university studies and received the tonsure, which conferred minor orders and qualified them for positions within the Church or the civil administration, the traditional careers for young men of modest means who hoped to rise in the social scale. Already beginning to recover from the desolation of famine, factional strife and English occupation, Paris, with its famous university, attracted considerable numbers of such students; and indeed, as Villon recognizes, some did indeed rise to positions of influence and affluence (T 233–40). But the supply of clerks was always greater than the demand for them, and social mobility could be downward as well as upward. Thus the city's population included an unhealthily large percentage of relatively well-educated but more or less unemployed graduates, living from a variety of precarious expedients while waiting for appointments that never came. As court records show, it was a recipe for rowdiness that could degenerate into serious crime. Many among Villon's immediate audience, therefore, would have shared not only his literary culture, but also his fear of justice, his distrust of authority, his constant anxiety over money, his bitter resentments, his need to find relief in sensual gratification and, above all, his deep sense of failure.

The Legacy

The *Legacy* contains an account of its own composition. It was, we are told, written at Christmas 1456, when the poet decided to leave for Angers in order to escape from an unhappy love affair. The conclusion tells us that the poem could not be completed because, after a trance induced by the bell of the Sorbonne, the poet found himself in the dark and could write no more. This self-refuting statement should be enough to undermine any naive faith a reader might have in the poem as autobiography. Villon did, in fact, leave Paris at Christmas 1456, but it was to put himself at a safe distance from justice after his participation in the robbery at the Collège de Navarre. Villon, in any case, is quick to bring in iconoclastic imagery that undoes his initial fashionable pose as a Petrarchan martyr to love: if now "some other distaff helps her weave" (L 52), he himself is off to "mint upon another die / And look for some fresh field to plough" (L 31–32).

Travel in the violent world of fifteenth-century France was often considered so dangerous as to justify the making of a precautionary will. Thus it is the prospect of a journey that provides the *Legacy* with a pretext for shifting genres from the traditional farewell to love which it initially parodies to the testamentary poem inherited from Jean de Meung and Eustache Deschamps. The list of bequests, which must have been a good deal funnier when it did not require annotation, relies for its effects on a cunning blend of the impossibly grandiose with the trivial or worthless, the subtly suitable and the wildly inappropriate. Guillaume de Villon, for example, is offered the somewhat dubious gift of the poet's fame, together with a non-existent lordly pavilion (L 69–72). Ythier Marchant and Jean le Cornu inherit a sword whose associations are phallic rather than chivalric, and whose value can be gauged by the fact that it has to be redeemed from the pawnshop for seven sous (L 81–88). There is a great deal of play with the allusive possibilities of house signs, whose apparent mobility reflects what seems to have been a common student prank. Some particularly derisive bequests are made possible by Villon's pet device of antiphrasis: thus the three destitute orphans who are given four farthings each or a share in the poet's non-existent property turn out to be three aged usurers (L 193–208), and the poor clerks to whom he transfers his university qualifications are rich and respectable canons of Notre-Dame (L 209–24). The targets are fairly predictable: corrupt lawyers and officials at the Châtelet, crooked policemen, avaricious financiers and tradesmen, social climbers with pretentions to aristocracy, overfed and lecherous friars. There is relatively little of the personal animus that will sharpen so many portraits in the *Testament*: only with the strangely anonymous character who is threatened with St Anthony's fire (L 261–64) does Villon suggest a personal motive for his hostility.

There is no consensus about why Villon chose to end his poem with a fictional trance. It has been suggested that he is claiming (or parodying) something like a *furor poeticus*, the rapture in which a poet receives inspiration – though in that case one would have expected the trance to function as an introduction rather than a conclusion. Or perhaps, as a recent graduate, he was simply glad to find a pretext for mocking the academic jargon that was the psychobabble of his time. A more intriguing suggestion is that Villon is offering an oblique excuse for his participation in the robbery as a passing moment of mental aberration; but he could just as well have invented the trance as a half-serious alibi to prove that, when the crime was committed, he was at home in Saint-Benoît.

The *Legacy* was probably started around the time of Villon's departure from Paris and completed fairly quickly. By the time Villon returned to the city in 1462, the poem had already achieved a certain notoriety (T 753–60) that must have guaranteed an audience for the greater achievement of the *Testament*.

The Testament

Whether the *Legacy* is or is not as unfinished as it claims to be, the *Testament* is a good deal more than its continuation or sequel. Composed shortly after Villon's liberation from the prison at Meung in 1461 and probably incorporating some material written earlier, it uses for the most part the same stanza of eight octosyllabic lines, relies on the same testamentary framework and takes a second stab at almost all the characters of the earlier work. The old formula, however, is not only revisited but revitalized in a number of crucial ways – by the insertion, at irregular intervals, of ballades and rondeaux that can be understood with little or no inside knowledge; by a dramatic variety of voices; by frequent shifts of tone that contribute to the construction of a highly ambiguous persona.

The Villon who returns to Paris in 1462 is obviously a more accomplished poet than the Villon who left five years earlier; he is also a man who has been wounded in body and mind by the privations and humiliations inflicted on him at Meung. It is the combination of technical progress with traumatic personal experience that explains the considerable development that the new poem gives to the basic testamentary form. In the *Legacy* this receives no more than the limited attention needed for it to function as a pretext for the exercise of Villon's comic verve; but in the *Testament* all the documentary formalities are punctiliously observed. We are told how the will relates to the previous bequests of the *Legacy* and where it is to be published; we learn who are to be its executors; we receive detailed instructions as to the funeral, the burial and the epitaph. Moreover, the very act of making the will is vividly recreated as we see the poet lying on his deathbed, prematurely aged, racked by thirst, coughing up balls of phlegm and dictating his last wishes to the sleepy fictive clerk Fremin. What all this attention to detail suggests is that the testament is not simply a handy device that gives free rein to Villon's satire: the parodic precision may be witty, but it cannot be light-hearted, for it is related to the thematic centre of the poem, which is a meditation on death as a physical event and on the fear of death as it conditions life. It is in this light that we should read the huge parenthesis that begins near the end of the first stanza and lasts for almost eight hundred lines before he gets down to the testament itself. Villon uses that long interval, sometimes called the *Regrets*, to examine his past life, to contemplate the ruinous effects of ageing and to reflect on his own mortality – in short, to put himself in the proper state of mind for making a will.

It cannot be doubted that "the harsh prison of Meung" had given Villon good reason to prepare himself for an early death; but the composition of a verse testament could also be used paradoxically as the promise of a new life. After the years of exile, Villon seems to be using the *Testament* to announce a break with the past and plead for social reintegration. Having been given a second chance by the King, to whom he offers undying loyalty, he now presents himself as a reformed character who has been chastened by recent experience, regrets his former dissipation and is newly vowed to celibacy. This is the persona we also recognize as *povre Villon*, more sinned against than sinning, guilty of little more than youthful over-exuberance and excessively punished for sowing a few wild oats. The poet's contemporaries may not have found it very convincing. The inner circle, at least, of Villon's audience would have noted that this portrait of a relatively harmless rascal makes no mention of the Sermoise affair or of the Collège de Navarre robbery: as they read the poet's self-pitying account of his sufferings in the prison at Meung, they might well have asked (as we still do) what crime brought him there in the first place. Villon, in any case, has a fierce resentment and an irrepressible vitality that keep returning to disturb the stance of deathbed penitent or pitiable victim. Thus the ballade in which he begs forgiveness of all men ends with thunderous curses against Thibaud d'Aussigny and his henchmen (T 1984–95), and the poet expires, not with a prayer, but with a near-miraculous erection and a last swig of dark red wine (T 2012–23).

The problem is that there are simply too many personae jostling for attention in the *Testament* – the deathbed penitent, the reformed sinner, the victim of poverty, the amiable fool, the resentful satirist, the unfortunate lover, the defiant rake. In the long run, one suspects, there is no point in looking for the man behind the masks: the Villon of the *Testament* is defined only by the variety of masks he is capable of assuming.

The sense of a speaker who frustrates all attempts to pin him down is reinforced by the ballades and rondeaux. Many of these may have been written earlier than the bulk of the text and, though some are linked to the testamentary structure by being offered as gifts to specific recipients (Villon's mother, Ythier Marchant, Robert d'Estouteville, Fat Margot), their insertion is often rather awkward. Nevertheless, in the amorous or erotic field especially, they challenge the reader by offering a number of options, none of which the poem as a whole seems to endorse. Thus we range from the monitory catalogue of biblical and classical figures destroyed by lust (T 625–72) to the wistful evocation of the beauties of past time (T 329–56), from the squalor of the brothel (T 1591–1627) to the luxurious sensuality of the canon and his dame Sidoine (T 1473–1506), from the harsh mercenary impera- tives of the girls on the game (T 533–60) to the perfect married love of Robert d'Estouteville and Ambroise Delor (T 1378–1405). Ultimately, perhaps, what lies behind this variety is Villon's desire to show that he has absorbed and modified most if not all of the genres and registers available to him. Taken together, the ballades and rondeaux constitute something like an embedded personal anthology, serving the two not incompatible purposes of poetic testament and self-advertisement.

Even a very short account of the *Testament* cannot conclude without some comment on Villon's almost incessant wordplay. This, of course, is an aspect of the poem that no translation can convey to any great extent, though it may make some gestures in the right direction. Take, for instance, *Je ne suis son serf ne sa biche* (T 12): here *serf* (serf) is a homophone pun with *cerf* (stag) and leads on to *biche* (doe), which is a common term of endearment addressed to women. Villon denies that Thibaud d'Aussigny has any authority over him and at the same time implies that the bishop has homosexual tendencies. Here, if we allow the archaic term "hind" (servant, but also deer), English can get fairly close to the original pun: "I'm not his hind, his little deer". But what is one to do with *menger d'angoisse mainte poire* (T 740)? Here the punning involves the literal pears from Angoisse in the Dordogne, the figurative bitter fruit of suffering (pears of anguish), and the pear-shaped metal gag or "chokepear" used as an instrument of torture. Finally, in the line where Villon declares that he loves the bishop's henchmen all equally, *Ainsi que fait Dieu le Lombart* (T 752), the syntax makes subject and object interchangeable: "the way God loves the Lombard" or "the way the Lombard loves God". The Lombards, regarded as the most unscrupulous bankers of the age, could hardly be said to show much love for God, and God presumably returns the compliment. In the context of equal love, however, *le Lombard* may also be Peter Lombard, the twelfth-century theologian who, in his famous *Sentences*, insisted on the indissoluble unity of the three persons in the Holy Trinity. There is not much a translator can do with this beyond settling for what seems to be the primary sense.

Though Marot was right to stress how much Villon's wit assumes the kind of knowledge that only his contemporaries could possess, one is inclined to doubt whether even the best-informed and most sophisticated of Villon's original readers could have grasped all these subtleties. For them, as for us, there would always have been a hint of something still obscure, some new incentive to exegetical ingenuity. There can be no doubt that this was intentional. When, towards the end of the poem, Villon confers on Jean de Calais, whom he has never met, the right to gloss, annotate, interpret and make sense of what he has written (T 1844–59), he is surely inviting his readers to enjoy the same freedom. The demands that the *Testament* makes on its audience are both flattering and teasing; it is not the only text where that combination has proved a powerful recipe for success.

Miscellaneous Poems

There has been much debate as to the chronology and authenticity of the *Miscellaneous Poems* (*Poésies diverses*), and the titles that have been attached to specific poems can often prove misleading. The fifteen poems in this volume are, however, accepted by all Villon's modern editors and can be arranged in four groups. The first and surely least interesting is composed of P i, ii and iii. Linked by their relentless anaphora and proverbial manner, these poems come across as juvenile and mechanical rhetorical exercises. Even the refrain "I know all things except myself" (P iii), sometimes seen as an anticipation of the unstable personality revealed in *The Legacy*, is in fact a sententious commonplace. Another group (P IV, V, VI) may be assigned to the poet's stay at the court of Charles d'Orléans at Blois in 1458. 'Ballade from the Contest at Blois' (P IV) is the third of a series of ten poems by various hands, all using the same opening line from a ballade by the Duke himself. What is striking is how the familiar "contradictions" or paradoxes of Petrarchan love poetry are used by Villon (in a way that anticipates Thomas Wyatt in England) to illustrate his own problematic status at the court – a situation summed up in one of those memorable refrains of which Villon has the secret: "Made welcome, and by all men turned away". The 'Praise of Marie d'Orléans' (P V) is Villon's attempt to establish himself as a court poet, a celebration of the birth of the Duke's daughter in terms that blend high-flown Marian imagery with explicit reference to Virgil's messianic fourth eclogue. As for the begging letter of 'Request to the Prince' (P VI), one can hardly imagine that familiar tone being used to any princely recipient other than a fellow poet.

Rather more hypothetical is the grouping of five poems that reflect Villon's captivity at Meung and its aftermath. The 'Letter to His Friends' (P VII), more likely to be a recollection than a genuine plea for help, combines a grim picture of the harsh prison conditions with a fine irony, for it was precisely the carefree lifestyle of his bohemian friends that made them unlikely to do much for him: they have as much chance of obtaining a pardon as of hoisting him out in a basket. The 'Debate between Villon and his Heart' (P VIII) is generally considered to date from the same period and derives from a long tradition of allegorical debate poems. Here the heart plays the role of conscience vainly seeking to awake a sense of personal responsibility in the poet, who takes refuge in a fatalism that also finds expression in 'Problem' (P XI), where Fortune is not so much fickle as implacably hostile. Two other poems have been plausibly assigned to the immediate post-Meung period on the grounds of affinities with the *Testament*: the patriotic exuberance of the 'Ballade against the Enemies of France' (P XI) is in keeping with the hyperbolic praise of Louis XI (T 56–72), while the 'Ballade of Good Counsel' (P X) recalls those in which the reformed rake insists on lecturing his old friends (T 1668–1719). The fourth and last group is composed of three poems related to Villon's condemnation and reprieve after the Ferrebouc affair in 1462–63. There is no cause to doubt that the wry little 'Quatrain' (P XIII) was actually written while Villon was awaiting execution and, by remarking that François is a "hard name to bear", Villon is probably expressing the not unreasonable view that his death sentence owes more to his reputation than to the real gravity of the crime. Both 'Praise and Request of the Court' (P xiv) and 'Question to the Prison Clerk' (xv) celebrate the success of his appeal to Parlement, perhaps all the more sweet because the reprieve was granted by a civil court rather than by the reputedly more lenient ecclesiastical justice from which he had been excluded.

There remains Villon's most famous poem, traditionally known as the 'Ballade of the Hanged Men' (P xii) and sometimes misleadingly entitled 'Villon's Epitaph'. It has often been read as a direct response to the death sentence, but, as the *Testament* amply demonstrates, Villon hardly needed that event to inspire him with the fear of hanging or the horror of physical decay. Moreover, the plural subject distinguishes it from the three first-person poems of the 1462–63 group. A poem that has received so much attention and that, in any case, speaks so directly needs no extensive commentary here. One would only wish to point out the subtle movement back and forth between particular and general, difference and similarity. The audience addressed as "human brothers who live after us" may seem initially to indicate some broad posterity, but narrows rapidly to the immediate contemporary onlookers who contemplate the rotting corpses swaying in the wind, only to broaden out again as the fate of the hanged men is seen to resemble our own. The warning not to "join our confraternity" marks a gap between the law-abiding citizens and the criminal community, but the emphasis on physical decay reminds us that, in the long run, we shall indeed all belong to the same brotherhood, with the same desperate need for God's mercy. The refrain "But pray to God that He forgive us all" gains in resonance and intensity: it starts out in a specific occasion as a plea from the hanged men who urge the living onlookers to intercede with God on their behalf; by the end of the poem it has become the vast supplication of fallen humanity praying for itself.

Villon in English

Villon's current reputation in the English-speaking world stands higher than that of any other French poet, with the exception of Baudelaire. Awareness of Villon began as early as 1823 with a *London Magazine* article by Henry Francis Cary (the translator of Dante); but what has been called the Villon cult, reflecting the Villon revival in France itself, did not get under way until the 1860s and '70s, with a whole series of essays and translations culminating in John Payne's *Poems of Master Francis Villon* (1878), first privately published and later made available to the general public in an expurgated edition (1881). Payne deserves credit for producing the first serious English translation of Villon, but the period's more lasting tribute to Villon is to be found in the work of Dante Gabriel Rossetti and Swinburne. Rossetti adapted Villon to his own brand of wistful medievalism, as can be seen in the three translations that he included in his *Poems* (1870): 'To Death, of His Lady', 'His Mother's Service to Our Lady', and, of course, 'The Ballad of Dead Ladies' with the inspired neologism that has made its refrain ("But where are the snows of yester-year?") as unforgettable in English as it is in French. But Rossetti's major work as a translator was with early Italian poetry, and his interest in Villon was never more than marginal. This is not the case with Swinburne, whose twelve versions of Villon cover a wider range and demonstrate a far deeper engagement. He responds not only to Villon's lyricism, but also, as the following extracts suggest, to his colloquial vigour and the uncompromising harshness of his vision.

> But soon the devil's among us flesh and fell,
> When penniless to bed comes Madge my whore;
> I loathe the very sight of her like hell.
> I snatch gown, girdle, surcoat, all she wore,
> And tell her, these shall stand against her score.
> She grips her hips with both hands, cursing God,
> Swearing by Jesus' body, bones, and blood,
> That they shall not. Then I, no whit dismayed,
> Cross her cracked nose with some stray shiver of wood
> Inside this brothel where we drive our trade.
>
> . . . .
> Ravens and pies with beaks that rend and rive
> Have dug our eyes out, and plucked off for fee
> Our beards and eyebrows; never are we free,
> Not once, to rest; but here and there still sped,
> Drive at its wild will by the wind's change led.

Villon's poetry obviously suited Swinburne's personal programme in that it challenged Victorian ideas of decorum in terms of subject matter, but this is not where the distinction of these versions really lies. Swinburne's own poetry is rarely as good as this. The sheer discipline of translation, the need to organize a given content within a fixed stanza form, Villon's avoidance of extended description and his precise concrete vocabulary – all these things curbed Swinburne's habitual verbosity, repetitiveness and over-indulgence in euphony as an end in itself. The resulting success demonstrates many of the qualities that would set Villon among the great models for the Modernists, thanks largely to the powerful advocacy of Ezra Pound.

In the new poetics that Pound sought to develop during the first decades of the twentieth century, Villon's work occupies a central position, because it is seen as embodying the two essential and related Modernist values of realism and economy. Realism is not, in this context, a question of subject matter. Villon's poetry is not "realistic" because it presents an accurate picture of Paris in the mid-fifteenth century or because it spends more time on whores and brothels than on, let's say, romantic love. Villon's realism is a quality of regard: as Pound puts it in *The Spirit of Romance* (1910), he has "the stubborn persistency of one whose gaze cannot be deflected from the actual fact before him" and who "holds his unique place in literature because he is the only poet without illusions". This absence of illusion becomes a stylistic virtue insofar as it leads to a direct unadorned language which contrasts with what Pound saw as the decorative or flowery manner of the Renaissance. In much the same vein, in *The Sacred Wood* (1921) T.S. Eliot classifies Villon among those poets whose greatness lies in "a peculiar honesty… against which the whole world conspires, because it is unpleasant": it is an honesty that is not concerned with the transitory ills of any given epoch, but only with "those things that exhibit the essential sickness or strength of the human soul" and it "never exists without great technical accomplishment". For both Pound and Eliot Villon functioned as an antidote to what they saw as the fatal Miltonic and Tennysonian flaws of magniloquence, abstraction and vagueness. Under the influence of Pound after 1911, W. B. Yeats also turned to Villon as an example of the pithy dramatic speech that he hoped would characterize the new Irish literature and that was achieved in his own movement away from the expansive dreamy lyricism of the Celtic Twilight to the spare and hard-edged rhetoric of his maturity.

Given Pound's insistence on translation as an essential training for poets, it is rather disappointing to see that this period did not produce any significant version of Villon, though Pound himself, when not hampered by an irritating pastiche-medieval diction, makes a powerful impression in the two "Villonaud" poems of *Personae* (1909):

> Lips shrunk back for the wind's caress
> As lips shrink back when we feel the strain
> Of love that loveth in hell's disdeign,
> And sense the teeth through lips that press
> 'Gainst our lips for the soul's distress
> That striveth to ours across the pain.
> ('A Villonaud: Ballad of the Gibbet')

Pound's archaisms are, in any case, less disturbing than the idiosyncratic Hiberno-English prose of the two Villon versions in J.M. Synge's *Poems and Translations* (1909). But probably the most enduring fruit of Pound's enthusiasm for Villon comes not from his own work, but from two early poems of his English disciple Basil Bunting. *The Well of Lycopolis* (1935) opens with a lively free-verse translation of the "Regrets of the Fair Armouress" and *Villon* (1925) is almost a collage of passages adapted from the *Testament*:

> Remember, imbeciles and wits,
> sots and ascetics, fair and foul,
> young girls with tender little tits,
> that DEATH is written over all.
> Worn hides that scarcely clothe the soul
> they are so rotten and so thin,
> or firm and soft and warm and full –
> fellmonger Death gets every skin.

No major poet since the Thirties has been as deeply and creatively engaged with Villon as were Pound and Bunting. In England the testamentary fiction reappeared in 'Auden and MacNeice: Their Last Will and Testament' in *Letters from Iceland* (1937), while George Barker borrowed the stanza-form of the *Testament* and appealed to Villon ("frank villain") to guide him in his rollicking *True Confession of George Barker* (1950). In America there have been some deft translations by Richard Wilbur, together with the more challenging versions of Robert Lowell. In *Imitations* (1961) Lowell lends his habitual verbal energy to the 'Ballade of the Hanged Men' ("Magpies / and crows have chiselled out our eyes, / have jerked away our beards and hair"), but weakens the effect with modish moralizing ("Oh brothers, you live after us / because we shared your revenue", "We hang in chains to satisfy / your justice and your violence"). In Britain the most notable contribution has been that of Tom Scott, whose much admired *Seeven Poems O Maister Francis Villon* (1953) shows how well Villon comes across in the language of Dunbar and Henryson:

> Tell me whaur, in whit countrie
> Bides Flora nou, yon Roman belle?
> Whaur Thais, Alcibiades be,
> Thon sibbit cuisins: can ye tell?
> Whaur clettaran Echo draws pell-mell
> Abuin some burn owrehung wi bine
> Her beautie's mair nor human spell –
> Ay, whaur are the snawes o langsyne?

Today it might seem that awareness of Villon among English-language poets is becoming limited to about half a dozen set pieces. There have, nonetheless, been a number of more or less complete recent translations. If we exclude Barbara Sargent-Baur (1994), an academic who explicitly renounces any ambition to produce English poetry, we are left with Galway Kinnell (1965) and Peter Dale (1973), two practising poets who differ widely in their attitude to verse translation. Kinnell believes that rhyme and metre "have become a dead hand, which it is just as well not to lay on any poetry" and translates accordingly in a laid-back fashion that is clear and readable but inevitably lacks Villon's stanzaic agility and epigrammatic force. Dale hopes that his work will "open again the possibility of strict metrical translation" and offers a virtuoso display of rhyming that is exhilarating even when it sounds over-ingenious. Both versions have virtues and shortcomings that, after forty years, should encourage and justify a new attempt.

Select Bibliography

ENGLISH

Translations:

Dale, Peter, *François Villon: Poems* (London: Anvil, 2001)

Kinnell, Galway, *The Poems of François Villon* (New York: Signet, 1965)

Sargent-Baur, Barbara, ed. and tr., *François Villon: Complete Poems* (Toronto: University of Toronto Press, 1994)

Commentary:

Fein, David, *François Villon and His Reader* (Detroit: Wayne State University Press, 1989)

Freeman, Michael, *François Villon in His Works: the Villain's Tale* (Amsterdam: Rodopi, 2000)

Hunt, Tony, *Villon's Last Will: Language and Authority in the 'Testament'* (Oxford: Clarendon, 1996)

Pound, Ezra, "Montcorbier, *alias* Villon", in *The Spirit of Romance* (London: Peter Owen, 1970)

Taylor, Jane H. M., *The Poetry of François Villon* (Cambridge: Cambridge University Press, 2001)

FRENCH

Editions:

Dufournet, Jean, *François Villon: Poésies* (Paris: Gallimard, 1988, *Collection Poésie 96*)

Rychner, Jean and Henry, Albert, *Le Testament Villon, texte et commentaire*, 2 vols (Geneva: Droz, 1974); *Le Lais Villon et les poèmes variés, texte et commentaire*, 2 vols (Geneva: Droz, 1977); *Index des mots, Index des noms propres, Index analytique* (Geneva: Droz, 1985)

Thiry, Claude, *François Villon: Poésies complètes* (Paris: Livre de poche, 1991)

Commentary:

Burger, André, *Lexique complet de la langue de Villon*, 2nd ed (Geneva: Droz, 1974)

Demarolle, Pierre, *Villon, un testament ambigu* (Paris: Larousse, 1973)

Dufournet, Jean, *Nouvelles recherches sur François Villon* (Paris: Champion, 1980)

Dufournet, Jean, *Villon, ambiguïté et carnaval* (Paris: Champion, 1992)

Geremek, Bronisław, *Les Marginaux parisiens aux XIVe et XVe siècles* (Paris: Flammarion, 1976)

Mus, David, *La Poétique de François Villon* (Seyssel: Champ Vallon, 1992)

Le Gentil, Pierre, *Villon* (Paris: Hatier, 1967)

Siciliano, Italo, *François Villon et les thèmes poétiques du Moyen Age* (Paris: Nizet, 1934)

Index of Names,
Places and Texts

Abelard, Peter [Esbaillart] (T 339): A controversial philosopher and theologian (1079–1142), he seduced and then married his brilliant pupil Héloïse, but was seized and castrated on the orders of her uncle Fulbert, canon of Notre-Dame. Both Abelard and Héloïse withdrew to lead separate religious lives. Their letters have survived.

Aeolus [Yolus] (P IX, 34): God of the winds.

Alençon, Duke of (T 383): Died in 1315 at the Battle of Agincourt.

Alexander (T 129; 162; P XI, 25): The story of Alexander and Diomedes seems to come from the fourth-century writer Julius Valerius, whom Villon confuses with the first-century historian Valerius Maximus. Alexander's desire to conquer the stars is reported in the medieval *Roman d'Alexandre*.

Alfonso (T 360): King of Aragon, d.1458. See also *Calixtus*.

Alice (T 347): Heroine of chronicle poetry (*chansons de geste*).

Alphasar (P XI, 28): Arphaxad, King of the Medes, was defeated and killed by Nebuchadnezzar (Judith 1:1–15).

Amnon (T 649): The son of David, he raped his sister Tamar and was killed by his brother Absalom (Samuel 13:6–29).

Angelot (T 1654): Herbalist in the parish of Saint-Germain-le-Vieux.

Angers (L 43): Town in western France, seat of the court of René d'Anjou, Villon's first stop in his wanderings after the Collège de Navarre robbery (1456).

Anthony, St (L 263, T 600). Hermit from Upper Egypt (*c.*250–336), invoked in cases of the skin disease known as St Anthony's fire (erysipelas).

Archipiada (T 331): A deformation of the name Alcibiades. The transformation of the Greek general into a beautiful woman resulted from a misreading of a passage in Boethius's *Consolation of Philosophy.*

Architriclinus (T 1243): Literally "master of the feast" in the Vulgate version of John 2:1–10 (the marriage feast at Cana). In Villon's time the term was misread as the name of the bridegroom.

Arembourg [Haranburgis] (T 348): Twelfth-century countess of Anjou and Maine.

Armouress, Fair [La Belle Heaulmière] (T 454): Almost certainly a fictional employment designed to avoid harassment by the authorities. An "armouress" is cited in a document of 1393 as mistress to Nicolas d'Orgemont, financier and canon of Notre-Dame.

Art of Memory (L 112): One of many Latin texts (*Ars memorativa, Ars memoriæ*) teaching basic mnemonic principles.

Arthur the Breton [Artus] (T 362): Died in 1458. Constable of France, he was prominent in the fight against England. See *Calixtus.*

Aussigny, Thibaud d' (T 6; 737): Bishop of Orléans and lord of Meung-sur-Loire, where, for reasons that remain obscure, Villon was imprisoned and deprived of his clerical status during the summer of 1461.

Auvergne, Dauphin of (T 382): Probably Béraud III, d.1426.

Averroës (T 96–97): Arab philosopher (1126–98) and author of an influential commentary on Aristotle.

Bailly, Jean de (T 1075): Clerk at the Treasury and solicitor in the Parlement, he lived near the Maubué fountain.

Basannier, Pierre (L 162; T 1362): Notary at the Châtelet, and later Clerk of the Court.

Bastard de la Barre: See *Marchant, Perrenet.*

Baude (T 1190): Baude de la Mare, a Carmelite friar who, if we believe Villon, kept a mistress and/or ran a brothel.

Beatrice [Bietrix] (T 347; P 11, 19): A heroine of chronicle poetry (*chansons de geste*).

Béguines (L 250; T 1159): Congregations of pious women who were self-supporting and did not take vows.

Bellefaye, Martin (T 1928): A lawyer at the Châtelet who held important offices under the Provost and served as counsellor to the court of Parlement. He is named as an executor in the *Testament*.

Bertha (T 347): Flat-footed Bertha is a folklore type, but Villon may be thinking of big-footed Bertha, the mother of Charlemagne, who, like Alice and Beatrice, appears in chronicle poetry.

Bicêtre (L 140; T 1347): A ruined castle in the Val-de-Marne.

Blanche (T 535): One of the Girls on the Game.

Blanche, Queen (T 345): Perhaps Blanche of Castille, mother of Saint Louis (Louis IX), but the *blanche* could well be an adjective, not a proper noun.

Blarru, Jean de (L 91): A wealthy Parisian goldsmith.

Bobignon, Pierre (T 995): A lawyer at the Châtelet, noted as a miserly landlord involved in litigation over gardens and houses that he refused to repair.

Bourbon, Charles, Duke of (T 361): Died of gout in 1456. See *Calixtus*.

Brunel Philippe (T 1941): See *Grigny*.

Bruyères, Mademoiselle de (T 1508): A pious woman, widow of Girard de Bruyères, treasurer of Charles VII; see *Devil's Fart*.

Buridan, Jean (T 342): Philosopher and rector of the University of Paris (1347). Student tradition celebrated his affair with the Queen of Navarre, who hid her habitual misconduct by disposing of her lovers in the way Villon recounts. Buridan escaped by placing a barge filled with hay under the palace windows. The legend seems to have confused the historical Jeanne de Navarre, wife of Philip IV, with her daughter-in-law Marguerite, the adulterous wife of Louis X.

Calais, Jean de (T 1845; 1952): A notary at the Châtelet, responsible for verifying wills.

Calixtus (T 357): Pope Calixtus III (r.1455–58) ordered a revision of the trial of Joan of Arc. T 357–64 provides a list of prominent figures who had died very recently, Villon's point being that they are no less dead than Charlemagne.

Capet, Hugh (P XV, 9): King of the Francs (r.987–96) and founder of the Capetian dynasty, said to be descended from a family of butchers.

Captain of the Watch [Chevalier du Guet] (L 145; T 1828): Jean de Harlay, commander of the Night Watch. His claim to knighthood was controversial.

Cardon, Jacques (L 123; T 1776): A rich Parisian draper. Villon mocks his gluttony and hints at problems with the law. His elder brother Jean was, like Guillaume de Villon, a chaplain at Saint-Benoît.

Carmelite Bull (L 95): A papal bull of 1409 giving the Mendicant orders, including the Carmelites, the right to hear confessions.

Carmelites (L 255; T 1191): A monastic order founded on Mount Carmel in 1112 and approved by Pope Honorius III in 1224.

Carthusians [Chartreux] (T 238; 1575; 1968): A religious order founded by St Bruno in 1084, they were installed in the old and allegedly haunted manor of Vauvert by Louis IX (Saint Louis) in 1257.

Cato (P V, 106): The moralizing couplets attributed in Villon's time to the famous Roman statesman were actually the work of English clerics.

Cayeux, Colin de (T 1675): Villon's accomplice in the Collège de Navarre robbery, he later became a member of the infamous gang of Coquillards and was hanged in 1460. Some biographers of Villon suspect Cayeux of having seduced the poet into a life of crime.

Celestines (T 238; 1575; 1968): A branch of the Benedictine order, founded in 1294 by Pietro da Morrone (Pope Celestine V). The Celestines had a particularly well-endowed convent in Paris.

Chapelain, Jean (T 1836): One of the twelve officers of the Provost's guard at the Châtelet. Villon plays on his name to suggest that he might have a career in the Church.

Charles VII (T 363): King of France (r.1422–61), father of Louis XI.

Charruau, Guillaume (T 1023): Lawyer and fellow student of Villon.

treats antiphrastically as "poor clerks". They were hostile to the community of Saint-Benoît (see *Villon, Guillaume de*).

Courault, Andry (T 1457): A royal counsellor at the Treasury and advisor of René d'Anjou.

Cow (L 173): House sign.

Crowned Ox (L 172): Sign of a butcher in Rue de la Harpe.

Culdoe, Michel (T 1338): A rich bourgeois and financier who was close to Charles VII and occupied important municipal functions in Paris. Villon's spelling ridicules his name (*Cul d'Oue*: goose arse).

Cypriot king (T 369): Jean III de Lusignan, noted for his disastrous reign as king of Cyprus (1432–58).

Dauphin (T 70): Eldest son of the King of France. Louis XI is the "late Dauphin" in that he has only recently ascended the throne.

Denise (T 1234): A woman who apparently took legal action against Villon for laying a curse upon her.

De Profundis (T 974): Psalm 130 ("Out of the depths"), one of the penitential psalms.

Detusca (T 1194): Not identified, but possibly Jean Turquant, a friend of Guillaume de Villon and officer of the Provost. The context indicates that he was involved in enforcing anti-prostitution laws, to the great annoyance of Friar Baude.

Deus Laudem (T 48): Psalm 108 in the Vulgate.

Devil's Fart [Pet au diable] (T 858): A large stone outside the house of Mademoiselle de Bruyères, frequently moved by rioting students. Villon suggests that it might be the subject of a mock epic.

Dicemont, Robbeville (T 1671–72): My translation of Montpipeau and Ruel, obscure place names chosen by Villon to suggest gambling and theft.

Diomedes (T 130; 154): The pirate who debates with Alexander in a story that Villon wrongly attributes to Valerius Maximus.

Dominic, St (T 1774): Founder of the Order of Preachers (Dominicans), which was particularly active in extirpating heresy in the south of France.

Donatus (T 1284): Fourth-century Latin grammarian.

Egyptian woman (T 885): St Mary of Egypt, a former courtesan who converted and led a life of spectacular asceticism in the desert.

Eighteen Clerks [Dix et Huit Clercs] (T 1322): The name of a college intended for infirm clerks and dependent on the Chapter of Notre-Dame.

Elaine (1483): The wife of Franc Gontier in Philippe de Vitry's pastoral poem.

Eleven-Score Guard [Unze-Vingt Sergens] (T 1086): A police force of 220 men responsible to the Provost of Paris.

Estouteville, Robert d': He is never named, but is clearly indicated at L 163 and T 1369. As Provost of Paris, he was charged with keeping order in the capital, a task which, as Villon suggests, he embraced with considerable zeal, notably in his suppression of student riots in 1452–53. He married Ambroise de Loré, whose name figures in acrostic at the beginning of the ballade that Villon leaves to him (T 1378–1405). The poem should be read more as an attempt to gain favour than as a proof of personal acquaintance.

Fifteen Signs (L 254): Signs announcing the Last Judgement.

Fifteen Twenties [les Quinze–Vingts] (T 1728): A hospice for the blind in Rue Saint-Honoré; its inmates were licensed to beg.

Flora (T 330): Name of Roman courtesan in Plutarch and Juvenal.

Foundlings [Enfants trouvés] (T 1660): An orphanage founded in the early fifteenth century by the Chapter of Notre-Dame.

Four, Michault du (T 1079): A butcher and innkeeper, but also a police officer at the Châtelet, he helped to investigate the robbery at the Collège de Navarre

Fournier, Pierre (L 165; T 1030): A legal advisor to the community of Saint-Benoît who may also have acted as Villon's own lawyer.

Fremin (T 565; 779; 787): The fictitious clerk to whom Villon dictates his testament.

Galerne, Colin (T 1653): A barber and churchwarden in the parish of Saint-Germain-le-Vieux.

Garde, Jean de la (L 258; T 1354; 1919): A wealthy spice merchant and supplier of the Queen's household, he is named by Villon as bellringer for his funeral.

Garnier, Etienne (P xv, 1): As clerk or doorkeeper of the Châtelet prison, he was on one occasion imprisoned himself for allowing an inmate to escape.

Genevois (T 1360): Probably Pierre Genevois, a lawyer at the Châtelet who defended first the interests of Notre-Dame and then those of Saint-Benoît.

Girard, Perrot (T 1150): A barber of Bourg-la-Reine, just south of Paris.

Glass Bell (T 1904): A notoriously fragile bell at Notre-Dame, it would hardly have been tolled for someone like Villon.

Glaucus (P ix, 35): Sea god, brother of Aeolus.

Glover Girl [Gantière] (T 533): One of the Girls on the Game.

Goblet [Grand Godet] (T 1039): A tavern in Place de Grève, now Place de l'Hôtel-de-Ville.

Golden Pestle [Mortier d'Or] (L 257): As the sign of a grocer-apothecary, mortar and pestle lend themselves to sexual innuendo.

Gontier, Franc (T 1458): An idealized peasant who praises the simple life in a poem by Philippe de Vitry (1291–1362).

Gossuin, Girard (L 202; T 1275): Originally a corn-chandler and later a notary at the Châtelet, Gossuin speculated on salt. With Jean Marceau and Colin Laurens, he belongs to the trio of old usurers antiphrastically mocked by Villon as "poor orphans" (L 196).

Gouvieux (L 269): Village near Chantilly with toll road, castle and pond – by Villon's time all in a run-down state. See *Rousseville, Pierre de.*

Grand Turk (P ix, 14): Mehmed II, Ottoman Emperor (r.1451–81) and conqueror of Constantinople, was said to have used Christian slaves as draught animals.

Green Cage [caige vert] (T 1195): Sign of the house where Friar Baude keeps a mistress or runs a brothel. "Cage" *was* also a slang term for female genitals.

Grigny, Philippe Brunel, Seigneur de (L 137; T 1347; 1941): Criminal and extortionate lord of the village of Grigny near Paris, he is named by Villon as an executor in the *Testament*.

Guesclin, Bertrand de [Claquin] (T 381): 1320–80, Constable of France, renowned for his bravery and skill in the war against the English.

Gueutry, Guillaume (L 223; T 1313): Always behind with the rent owed to the chapter of Notre-Dame.

Guillemette (T 543): Carpet-weaver, a Girl on the Game.

Guillemette (T 1782): Figure in a bawdy song.

Helm (L 146): Sign of a tavern in Rue Saint-Jacques.

Héloïse [Esloÿs] (T 337): Lover of the philosopher Peter Abelard. See *Abelard*.

Henry (T 1643): Henri Cousin, an official charged with carrying out sentences such as hanging, flogging, etc.

Hesselin, Denis (T 1014): A tax collector, especially concerned with the wine trade.

Hôtel-Dieu (T 1644): An ancient hospital in the square before Notre-Dame, in Villon's time it housed up to 500 inmates in deplorable conditions.

Hussite heresy [faulte des Boesmes] (P 11, 22): A heretical movement in Bohemia and Moravia; its leader, Jan Hus, was condemned by the Council of Constance and burnt in 1415.

Innocents (T 1734): The largest Parisian cemetery. Enclosed by high walls, it contained eighty arcades with two levels, the upper containing the bones of those disinterred to make room for new burials. One wall was covered with frescos depicting the Dance of Death.

Jacoppins (L 159; T 1574): Name given to the Dominican order (Order of Preachers), translated here as *friars*.

James, Jacques (T 1812; 1944): Architect and owner of a disreputable bathhouse, he is named as an executor in the *Testament*.

Jane Bonneteer (T 549): A Girl on the Game.

Jeanne de Bretaigne (T 1629): A prostitute listed in documents of the period.

Joan of Lorraine [Jehanne] (T 349): Joan of Arc, a peasant girl who led the resistance to the English and was burnt as a heretic at Rouen in 1431. When Villon wrote his 'Ballade of the Ladies of Times Past', her rehabilitation (1456) was a very recent event.

Jolis, Noël (T 662; 1636): Probably Villon's rival for the favour of Kate Vausselles, but the incident recalled at T 657–64 remains obscure.

Juvenel, Michel (T 1934): A financier who held important offices in the royal household, he is named by Villon as an executor in the *Testament*.

Kate [Katherine de Vausselles] (T 661): Perhaps the mistress of Villon, perhaps to be identified with the "rose" of T 910. See *Jolis, Noël*.

Kate (T 551): Maker of purses, a Girl on the Game.

Keg [le Barillet] (T 1359): A tavern near the Châtelet.

Lancelot (T 378): Not the Arthurian Lancelot, but Ladislas V of Hungary and Bohemia, who died at the age of seventeen in 1457.

Lantern (L 150): House sign in Rue de la Pierre-au-Lait, behind the Châtelet.

Laurens, Colin (L 201; T 1275): Usurer, grocer, speculator and one of Villon's three "poor orphans" (L 196). See *Gossuin, Girard* and *Marceau, Jean*.

Laurens, Jean (T 1222): Prosecutor of the Paris diocese who helped to extract the confession of Guy Tabarie that implicated Villon in the Collège de Navarre robbery.

Lazarus [le Ladre] (T 816): The poor man in the parable of Dives and Lazarus (Luke 16:19-31). Not to be confused with the Lazarus whom Christ raised from the dead.

Lombard (T 752; P VI 22): Italian bankers, commonly known as Lombards, were generally regarded as unscrupulous usurers. At T 752 there may also be a pun on the name of the theologian Peter Lombard (1096–1164), whose *Sentences* were a standard textbook and who discussed the equality of persons within the Holy Trinity.

Lomer, Pierre (T 1796): A priest of Notre-Dame charged with the expulsion of certain prostitutes, but the bequest suggests that he might prefer to become their client.

Loré, Ambroise de (T 1378–91): Robert d'Estouteville's wife, whose name is given in acrostic.

Louis XI (T 56): King of France (r.1461–83), successor to Charles VII.

Loup, Jean le (L 185; T 1110): A police informer and racketeer, his repeated condemnations for criminal activities did not prevent him from ending up as a functionary at the Châtelet. See *Cholet, Casin.*

Louviers or *Louvieux, Nicolas de* (L 266; T 1047): A draper and financier who held a number of key political posts in Paris.

Macée [Macé d'Orléans] (T 1210): Bailiff of Berry, accused of extortion; Villon's feminization of his name implies sexual deviance.

Machecoue (T 1053): Seller of poultry and roast meats near the Châtelet.

Macquaire (T 1418): A comically bad cook in *The Martyrdom of St Bacchus* (1318) by Geoffroy de Paris.

Macrobius (T 1547): Fifth-century author of *Commentarii in somnium scipionis*, a celebrated commentary on Cicero.

Magdalen (P IX, 16): Villon seems to confuse Mary Magdalen with St Mary of Egypt. See *Egyptian woman.*

Malpensé (L 111): The personification of stupidity.

Marceau, Jean (L 202; T 1275): A usurer from Rouen and enemy of Robert d'Estouteville, he was eventually imprisoned for illegal financial dealings. One of Villon's "poor orphans" (L 196). See *Gossuin, Girard* and *Laurens, Colin.*

Marchant, Perrenet, Bastard de la Barre (L 177; T 764; 937; 1094): One of the twelve officers at the Châtelet charged with protecting the Provost. Villon presents him as a whoremonger and plays on his name to suggest the disreputable nature of his trade.

Marchant, Ythier (L 81; T 970; 1024): Born into a family of magistrates, he may have been a fellow student of Villon. After serving as a financial administrator for Charles de Guyenne, brother to the King, he was accused in 1474 of plotting against Louis XI and died in prison.

Marcquet (T 1830): Marcquet and Philibert are two aged police-men who have been dismissed by Tristan l'Hermite. Villon treats them antiphrastically as "little pages".

Margot [la Grosse Margot] (T 1583; 1602): Though Margot was a common name among prostitutes, this may well be the *Grosse Margot* who was involved with the criminal Regnier de Montigny, banished from Paris in 1452 for beating up two sergeants of the night watch outside her door. See *Montigny, Regnier de.*

Marie d'Orléans (P v): Daughter of Charles d'Orléans and Marie de Clèves, born in 1457.

Marion l'Idole (T 1628; 1663): Prostitute whose name, together with that of her pimp, occurs in legal documents of 1461.

Marle, (T 1266): Probably Germain de Marle, who had inherited his father's business as a money-changer.

Marthe (T 950–55): Name in acrostic, probably that of a lover of Villon.

Martial, St (T 69): Third-century Bishop of Limoges with nothing martial about him but the name.

Master of the Wills (T 1952): See *Calais.*

Mathurin, St (T 1280): Fourth-century saint, renowned for curing madness. Villon confuses him with St John of Matha (1169–1218) founder of the Trinitarian order known as Mathurins (*Mathelins*).

Matthew [Matheolus] (T 1179): Late-thirteenth-century author of the violently misogynistic *Liber lamentationum.*

Maubué (T 1076): Ancient fountain in Rue Saint-Martin.

Mautaint, Jean (L 161; T 1366): Notary at the Châtelet responsible for examining witnesses and investigating crimes, including the robbery at the Collège de Navarre.

Mendicants [Mendiants] (L 249; T 1158; 1649; 1969): The four religious orders vowed to poverty: Augustinians, Carmelites, Dominicans and Franciscans. There was bitter rivalry between the Mendicants and the secular clergy, who fought to maintain a monopoly over preaching and confession.

Merebeuf, Pierre de (L 265; T 1046): Rich draper, associated with Nicolas de Louviers.

Meun, Jean de (T 1178): Major thirteenth-century poet (*c.*1240–*c.*1305). See *Romance of the Rose*.

Meung (T 83; 1633): *Meung-sur-Loire*, small town west of Paris, where Villon was imprisoned in 1461.

Michault (T 922): Legendary figure said to have died from excessive amorous effort.

Millières, Jeanne de (L 104): Mistress of Robert Valée.

Montigny, Regnier de (L 130; 139): One of Villon's criminal friends, despite his noble birth. Guilty of murder and theft from churches, he joined the infamous band of the Coquillards and was hanged in 1457.

Montmartre (T 1551): Site of a convent, much decayed in Villon's time.

Montpipeau, Ruel (T 1671–72): See *Dicemont, Robbeville*.

Moreau, Jean (T 774): Seller of roast meats, a creditor of Villon, named as one of his three heirs. See *Provins* and *Turgis*.

Mouton or *Moutonnier* (L 142): Perhaps someone engaged in a lawsuit against the Seigneur de Grigny. Villon assumed the name Mouton when he was being treated for his wounds after the death of Philippe Sermoise.

Mule (L 90; T 1013): A tavern in Rue Saint-Jacques where Villon and his accomplices prepared their break-in at the Collège de Navarre.

Nijon (L 138): Ruined fortress between Chaillot and Passy.

Nine Orders (T 838): The Angelic Orders: Seraphim, Cherubim, Thrones, Dominations, Virtues, Powers, Principalities, Archangels, Angels.

Octavian's age (P IX, 23): Not the Octavian of history, but a legendary Roman emperor punished for his avarice by having molten gold poured down his throat.

Ogier [Auger le Danois] (T 1803): One of Charlemagne's paladins, but also linked to the Arthurian cycle where he is the lover of Morgan le Fay.

Parlement (L 98): Not so much a parliament in the modern sense as a judicial body applying royal justice.

Pactay (P VI, 17): Town eighty miles south-west of Paris. There were no woods around Pactay and hence no chestnuts.

Perdrier, Jean and François (T 1406–7): Sons of the money-changer Guillaume Perdrier, they both held lucrative posts in the royal administration.

Petit-Pont (T 1533): Bridge linking the Cité and the Left Bank.

Philibert (T 1830): See *Marcquet*.

Picard (T 37): Picardy had seen some persecution of heretics in 1459–60, but there was also an extreme Bohemian sect known as "Picardi".

Pine Cone [Pomme de Pin] (L 157; T 1045): A tavern in the Cité, Rue de la Juiverie; one of Villon's favourite haunts.

Poitou (T 1065): Region of western France; Villon imitates the local dialect in T 1062–69.

Pontoise (P XIII, 2): Small town twenty miles north-west of Paris.

Pouilli, Jean de (T 1174): A theologian of the University of Paris who opposed the Mendicant orders and denied their right to confess the faithful. In 1321 his theses were condemned by Pope John XXII and he was forced to recant.

Pourras (T 1157): The convent of Port-Royal, where the abbess was the debauched Huguette de Hamel, later imprisoned and deprived of her benefice.

Prince of Fools (L 272; T 1078): An official charged with organizing outdoor entertainments, he distributed comic imitation money.

Provins, Jean de (T 774): A pastry cook, one of Villon's creditors, named as his heir with Moreau and Turgis.

Provost Marshall (T 1833): Tristan l'Hermite, chief of the military police. See *Marcquet* and *Philibert*.

Raguier, Jacques (L 153; T 1038; 1943): Perhaps the son of Lubin Raguier, master of the royal kitchens, he was evidently a regular at the *Pine Cone* and is named by Villon as an executor in the *Testament*.

Raguier, Jean (L 131; T 1070): One of the twelve officers charged with protecting the Provost of Paris.

Red Ass (T 1013): Presumably another tavern sign.

René [Regnier] (T 1375): René d'Anjou inherited the kingdom of Sicily, which was soon lost to the Spanish. His writings in poetry and prose uphold the chivalric ideal. The tournament in which Robert d'Estouteville took part was held at Saumur in 1446.

Richier, Denis (T 1089): Officer of the Eleven-Score Guard.

Richier, Pierre (T 1283): Master of theology and schoolteacher.

Riou, Jean (T 1126): A wealthy furrier, captain of a largely decorative citizen force of 120 archers.

Rob [maistre Robert] (T 750): Torturer in the prison at Meung.

Romance of the Rose (T 113): Long and hugely influential poem in two parts: the first of 4,058 lines by Guillaume de Lorris, the second of 17,722 lines written forty years later (*c.*1268–85) by Jean de Meun, who takes a rational and sceptical view of courtly love. See Chaucer, *The Romaunt of the Rose.*

Rosnel, Nicolas (T 1366): An examiner at the Châtelet.

Rousseville, Pierre de (L 270): Warden of the run-down castle and fish ponds at Gouvieux.

Ru, Guillaume du (T 1961): Wine merchant.

Rueil, Jean de (T 1365): Auditor at the Châtelet; his brother Pierre was a spice merchant, hence Villon's mocking reference to cloves.

Sage (T 210; 1461): Author of the Book of Ecclesiastes, in Villon's time presumed to be Solomon.

Saint-Amant, Pierre de (L 89; T 1007): Prominent figure in the royal administration, secretary of Charles VII and Clerk of the Treasury from 1447. The name offers Villon a golden occasion to mock his presumed impotence and the sterility of his wife.

Saint-Antoine, Rue (L 226): In Villon's time the most important street in Paris.

Sainte-Avoie (T 1869): In Rue du Temple; originally home to a community of pious widows, but by the fifteenth century a hostel for fallen women.

Saint-Denis (T 339): Benedictine abbey, burial place of French kings.

Saint-Generou (T 1063): Saint-Généroux, village in department of Deux-Sèvres; not, in fact, near Saint-Julien-de-Voventes, which is more than sixty miles away. Villon may be punning with Parisian pronunciation: *Je ne soulds vos ventes* ("I won't pay your sales").

St James [Saint-Jacques] (L 120): There were booths for public scribes on the north side of this church near the Châtelet.

Saint-Omer (T 615): Town in the department of Pas de Calais.

Salins (T 403; 1278): Town in the Jura, chosen because its name (salt mines) recalls the traffic in salt of the three speculators that Villon presents as "poor orphans".

Sardana, Sardanapalus (T 641; P IX 32): Legendary king of Assyria, noted for his debauchery; defeated by a rebellion, he built a huge pyre and burned himself to death together with his concubines.

Scipio (P XI, 19): Scipio Africanus, who defeated Hannibal and was later exiled, but seems to have died a natural death. Villon may be confusing him with Scipio Emilianus, who destroyed Carthage in 146 BC and was probably poisoned in 129 BC.

Scots king (T 365): James II of Scotland, known as "Fiery Face" because of his birthmark, was killed by the explosion of a canon in 1460.

Seneschal (T 1820): Pierre de Brézé, Seneschal of Normandy and a heroic military leader against the English, fell out of favour for a time after the accession of Louis XI.

Sidoine (T 1475): Mistress of the fat canon in Villon's ballade "refuting Franc Gontier".

Simon Magus (P IX, 21): Sorcerer who attempted to buy the power of the Holy Ghost from the Apostles (Acts 8:9–24). The story of him levitating and then falling to his death is told in Jacopo da Voragine's *Golden Legend*.

Sorbonne (L 276): The famous university was only a few doors down from the cloister of Saint-Benoît, where Villon lodged until 1456. In L 281–304 Villon mocks the abstruse scholastic terminology prevalent at the Sorbonne and other universities.

Stephen, St [Etienne] (T 1915): Protomartyr, stoned to death (Acts 7–8). Small buns, perhaps recalling the stones, were distributed on his feast day.

Tabarie, Guy (T 859): Fellow student of Villon and his accomplice in the robbery at the Collège de Navarre. After indiscreet conversations with a priest who turned out to be an informer, he was arrested in 1458 and, under torture, confessed and named Villon. He was released on payment of fifty *écus*.

Tacque Thibaud (T 737): Corrupt favourite of Duke Jean de Berry.

Taillevant (T 1414): Master of the royal kitchen, author of a famous fourteenth-century cookbook.

Tarrenne, Charlot (T 1339): Financier and follower of Charles VII.

Templars (T 1029). The Order of Templars, suppressed in 1312. In Villon's time their enclosed land still lay waste on the outskirts of Paris and there would have been no pavement.

Thaïs (T 331): Either the mistress of Alexander or, more probably, the Egyptian courtesan converted to Christianity whose story is told in the *Golden Legend*.

Theophilus (T 886): A legendary clerk who signed a pact with the Devil, but was saved by the intervention of the Virgin Mary. Retold by the thirteenth-century poet Rutebeuf (*Miracle de Théophile*), the story was very popular and can be seen sculpted on the north portal of Notre-Dame.

Three Lily Buds [Troys Lis]: One of the prisons at the Châtelet.

Three poor orphans (T 1275): The three old usurers, Girard Gossuin, Jean Marceau and Colin Laurens.

Tricquot, Thomas (T 1955): Priest from Meaux who graduated in 1452 and may have been Villon's fellow student.

Trouscaille (T 1142): Robin Trascaille, tax collector and clerk at the Treasury. Villon suggests his debauchery by distorting his name into *Trouscaille* (Pressbird).

Trouvé, Jean (L 169): This assistant butcher at the Grande Boucherie was often in trouble with the law for his violent behaviour.

Turgis, Robin (T 774; 1017; 1054): Owner of the *Pine Cone*; named as Villon's creditor and heir with Moreau and Provins.

Turlupins, Turlupines (T 1161): A heretical sect, finally extirpated in *c*.1420. Their insistence on the goodness of all natural urges and their alleged practice of nudism led to accusations of promiscuity.

Vacquerie, François de la (T 1214): An ecclesiastical prosecutor involved in the investigation of the robbery at the Collège de Navarre. As a cleric he would not have been eligible for knighthood, and the incident that Villon alludes to remains obscure.

Valée, Robert (L 97; 114): A fellow student of Villon and a prosecutor in the Parlement, ironically presented as poor and in need of help. He is unlikely to have been as witless as Villon suggests.

Valerius (T 159–60): Valerius Maximus, first-century Latin historian. See *Alexander.*

Valérien (T 1554): The hill to the west of Paris offers Villon a pretext for punning – the nuns are worth nothing (*valent rien*).

Valette, Jean (T 1089): An officer of the Eleven-Score Guard.

Vauselles (T 661): See *Kate.*

Vauvert (T 1197): A ruined Parisian abbey, supposedly haunted by the Devil.

Vegetius (L 6): Fourth-century author of a treatise on military affairs, *Epitoma rei militaris.*

Victor, Saint (P IX, 26): Roman martyr, ground to death by millstones, *c.*300.

Villon, Guillaume de (L 70; T 850): Professor of canon law, chaplain at Saint-Benoît-le-Bétourné, adoptive father of Villon.

Vitry, Thibaud de (L 218; T 1306): Canon and benefactor of Notre-Dame. See *Cottin, Guillaume.*

Volant, Guillaume (T 1916): A noted public figure in Paris, he was the city's ambassador to Charles VII and grew rich in the salt trade. Villon names him as the bellringer at his funeral.

Woodsmith [Orfevre de Boys] (T 1118): The nickname of Jean Mahé, torturer at the Châtelet.

Index of First Lines in French

Index of First Lines in English

Acknowledgements

To the problems inherent in all verse translation Villon adds the difficulty of his fifteenth-century language, the obscurity of his contemporary reference and the density of his ambiguities. I am, therefore, more than usually indebted to the dedicated and fruitful scholarship of the editors and commentators listed in my bibliography, and especially to the late Michael Freeman who was uniquely sensitive to the resonance of Villon in English poetry. Among my early readers Gerard Rochford offered perceptive comment on my versions of the great set pieces while John E. Jackson has been generous with advice and encouragement – not only on this occasion, but throughout our long friendship. Richard Waswo can have no reason to read this book for a second time other than the pleasure of recognizing his own hand in its happier moments.

A selection of these translations appeared in *Literary Imagination* (Winter, 2013).

– Anthony Mortimer, 2013

Anthony Mortimer is Professor Emeritus of English Literature at the University of Fribourg, Switzerland, and also taught for many years at the University of Geneva. In addition to his scholarly work on Early Modern poetry, he has published a series of verse translations, including Petrarch's *Canzoniere* (2002) and Michelangelo's *Poems and Letters* (2007) for Penguin Classics; *The Sacred Epigrams* of Angelus Silesius (2013) for AMS, New York; Dante's *Rime* (with J.G. Nichols, 2009) and *Vita Nuova* (2011), the *Complete Poems* of Guido Cavalcanti (2019), Baudelaire's *Flowers of Evil* (2016) and *The Song of Roland* (2019) for Alma Classics.

EVERGREENS SERIES

Beautifully produced classics, affordably priced

Alma Classics is committed to making available a wide range of literature from around the globe. Most of the titles are enriched by an extensive critical apparatus, notes and extra reading material, as well as a selection of photographs. The texts are based on the most authoritative editions and edited using a fresh, accessible editorial approach. With an emphasis on production, editorial and typographical values, Alma Classics aspires to revitalize the whole experience of reading classics.

For our complete list and latest offers

visit

almabooks.com/evergreens

GREAT POETS SERIES

Each volume is based on the most authoritative text, and reflects Alma's commitment to provide affordable editions with valuable insight into the great poets' works.

Selected Poems
Blake, William
ISBN: 9781847498212
£7.99 • PB • 288 pp

The Rime of the Ancient Mariner
Coleridge, Samuel Taylor
ISBN: 9781847497529
£7.99 • PB • 256 pp

Complete Poems
Keats, John
ISBN: 9781847497567
£9.99 • PB • 520 pp

Paradise Lost
Milton, John
ISBN: 9781847498038
£7.99 • PB • 320 pp

Sonnets
Shakespeare, William
ISBN: 9781847496089
£4.99 • PB • 256 pp

Leaves of Grass
Whitman, Walt
ISBN: 9781847497550
£8.99 • PB • 288 pp

MORE POETRY TITLES

Dante Alighieri: *Inferno, Purgatory, Paradise, Rime, Vita Nuova, Love Poems*; Alexander Pushkin: *Lyrics Vol. 1 and 2, Love Poems, Ruslan and Lyudmila*; François Villon: *The Testament and Other Poems*; Cecco Angiolieri: *Sonnets*; Guido Cavalcanti: *Complete Poems*; Emily Brontë: *Poems from the Moor*; Anonymous: *Beowulf*; Ugo Foscolo: *Sepulchres*; W.B. Yeats: *Selected Poems*; Charles Baudelaire: *The Flowers of Evil*; Sándor Márai: *The Withering World*; Antonia Pozzi: *Poems*; Giuseppe Gioacchino Belli: *Sonnets*; Dickens: *Poems*

WWW.ALMABOOKS.COM/POETRY

ALMA CLASSICS

ALMA CLASSICS aims to publish mainstream and lesser-known European classics in an innovative and striking way, while employing the highest editorial and production standards. By way of a unique approach the range offers much more, both visually and textually, than readers have come to expect from contemporary classics publishing.

LATEST TITLES PUBLISHED BY ALMA CLASSICS

www.almaclassics.com